SHADOWS

Twenty-One Designs
By
Kim Hargreaves

CREDITS

DESIGNS & STYLING
Kim Hargreaves

EDITOR
Kathleen Hargreaves

MODEL
Naomi Vergette-D'Souza

HAIR & MAKE-UP
Diana Fisher

PHOTOGRAPHY & EDITORIAL DESIGN
Graham Watts

LAYOUTS
Angela Lin

PATTERNS
Sue Whiting & Trisha McKenzie

© Copyright Kim Hargreaves 2011

First published in 2011 by Kim Hargreaves
Intake Cottage, 26 Underbank Old Road, Holmfirth
West Yorkshire, HD9 1EA, England

British Library Cataloguing in Publication Data
A catalogue record for this book is available from the British Library

ISBN-10   1-906487-11-9
ISBN-13   978-1-906487-11-9

CONTENTS

OUT OF THE
SHADOWS

This season's bold boy-meets-girl chic makes a playful nod towards a light androgyny. The result, sharp silhouettes, masculine lines and tomboy tailoring, while addressing the balance are body hugging cables and supple ribs which both caress and celebrate feminine curves.

STEEL | SHEER CLOSE-FITTING SWEATER

ABLE | CLOSE-FITTING CABLED SKIRT WITH SHAPING DETAILS

KENT | RIBBED BOXY JACKET

LOGAN | LEAN CABLED TUNIC

WILL | ELEGANT CABLED CARDIGAN

SHARP | CHIC CROCHET JACKET WITH POCKET & EPAULETS

HARRIS | SMART COAT WITH EPAULETS & CROCHET EDGINGS

BLAKE | TIMELESS SLOPPY JOE

DEEP | STYLISH CABLED HAT

LOGAN | CLOSE-FITTING CABLED DRESS

THUNDER | CLASSIC CABLE & RIB SCARF   **ABLE** | BODY-HUGGING CABLED SKIRT

SETH | UNDERSTATED SWEATER WITH SHOULDER DETAIL

HANLEY | CLASSIC LONG-LINE SWEATER

CARTER | SOFT OVERSIZED SCARF

DERWIN | ELEGANT SWEATER WITH CABLES SET INTO RIB

BARON | EFFORTLESS BELTED PONCHO   DERWIN | CABLES & RIB SWEATER

FLETCHER | SNUG CABLED COAT

TOUGH | SEMI-FITTED JACKET WITH CABLES & GENEROUS COLLAR

BRAD | A-LINE CARDIGAN WORKED IN AN OPEN FABRIC

RUMBLE | UNDERSTATED STRIPED SWEATER

THE
PATTERNS

Recommendation

Suitable for the knitter with a little experience
Please see pages 7, 8 & 9 for photographs.

	XS	S	M	L	XL	XXL	
To fit	81	86	91	97	102	109	cm
bust	32	34	36	38	40	43	in

Rowan Kidsilk Haze

	6	7	7	7	8	8	x 25gm

Photographed in Hurricane

Needles

1 pair 3¼mm (no 10) (US 3) needles
1 pair 4mm (no 8) (US 6) needles
1 pair 4½mm (no 7) (US 7) needles
1 pair 7mm (no 2) (US 10½ /11) needles
1 pair 8mm (no 0) (US 11) needles
1 pair 9mm (no 00) (US 13) needles

Tension

12 sts and 19 rows to 10 cm measured over
pattern using a combination of 4½mm (US 7)
and 9mm (US 13) needles and yarn DOUBLE.

STEEL

Close-fitting sweater worked in an open fabric

BACK

Cast on 55 (57: 61: 63: 67: 71) sts using
9mm (US 13) needles and yarn DOUBLE.
Row 1 (RS): Using a 4½mm (US 7) needle,
knit.
Row 2: Using a 9mm (US 13) needle, purl.
These 2 rows form patt.
Work in patt for a further 14 rows, ending
with a WS row.
Row 17 (RS): K3, K2tog, K to last 5 sts, K2tog
tbl, K3.
Working all side seam decreases as set by last
row, dec 1 st at each end of 8th and 3 foll 8th
rows. 45 (47: 51: 53: 57: 61) sts.
Work 15 rows, ending with a WS row.
Row 65 (RS): K3, M1, K to last 3 sts, M1, K3.
Working all side seam increases as set by last
row, inc 1 st at each end of 10th and foll 10th
row. 51 (53: 57: 59: 63: 67) sts.
Cont straight until back measures 49 (49: 49:
50: 50: 50) cm, ending with a WS row.
Shape armholes
Cast off 3 sts at beg of next 2 rows.
45 (47: 51: 53: 57: 61) sts.
Dec 1 st at each end of next 1 (1: 1: 3: 3: 3)
rows, then on foll 2 (2: 3: 2: 3: 4) alt rows,
then on foll 4th row.
37 (39: 41: 41: 43: 45) sts.
Cont straight until armhole measures 18 (19:
20: 20: 21: 22) cm, ending with a WS row.
Shape shoulders and back neck
Next row (RS): Cast off 3 (3: 3: 3: 3: 4) sts,
K until there are 7 (7: 8: 7: 8: 8) sts on right
needle and turn, leaving rem sts on a holder.
Work each side of neck separately.
Cast off 4 sts at beg of next row.
Cast off rem 3 (3: 4: 3: 4: 4) sts.
With RS facing, rejoin yarn to rem sts, cast
off centre 17 (19: 19: 21: 21: 21) sts **loosely**,
K to end.
Complete to match first side, reversing shapings.

FRONT

Work as given for back until 14 rows less have
been worked than on back to start of shoulder
shaping, ending with a WS row.
Shape front neck
Next row (RS): K12 (12: 13: 12: 13: 14)
and turn, leaving rem sts on a holder.
Work each side of neck separately.

Dec 1 st at neck edge of next 4 rows, then
on foll alt row, then on foll 4th row.
6 (6: 7: 6: 7: 8) sts.
Work 3 rows, ending with a WS row.
Shape shoulder
Cast off 3 (3: 3: 3: 3: 4) sts at beg of next row.
Work 1 row.
Cast off rem 3 (3: 4: 3: 4: 4) sts.
With RS facing, rejoin yarn to rem sts, cast off
centre 13 (15: 15: 17: 17: 17) sts loosely,
K to end.
Complete to match first side, reversing
shapings.

SLEEVES (both alike)

Cast on 24 (26: 28: 28: 30: 30) sts using 9mm
(US 13) needles and yarn DOUBLE.
Beg with a K row using 4½mm (US 7) needle
and working all increases in same way as side
seam increases, work in patt as given for back,
shaping sides by inc 1 st at each end of 17th
and 2 (3: 4: 5: 5: 6) foll 14th rows, then on
4 (3: 2: 1: 1: 0) foll 12th rows.
38 (40: 42: 42: 44: 44) sts.
Cont straight until sleeve measures 52 (53: 54:
55: 56: 57) cm, ending with a WS row.
Shape top
Cast off 3 sts at beg of next 2 rows.
32 (34: 36: 36: 38: 38) sts.
Dec 1 st at each end of next row, then on foll
alt row, then on 3 (3: 3: 3: 3: 4) foll 4th rows.
22 (24: 26: 26: 28: 26) sts.
Work 1 row, ending with a WS row.
Dec 1 st at each end of next and every foll alt
row to 18 sts, then on foll 3 rows, ending with
a WS row.
Cast off rem 12 sts.

MAKING UP

Press all pieces with a warm iron over
a damp cloth.
Join right shoulder seam using back stitch
or mattress stitch if preferred.
Collar
With RS facing, using 7mm (US 10½ /11)
needles and yarn DOUBLE, pick up and knit 16
sts down left side of neck, 13 (15: 15: 17: 17:
17) sts from front, 16 sts up right side of neck,
then 25 (27: 27: 29: 29: 29) sts from back.
70 (74: 74: 78: 78: 78) sts.

Row 1 (RS of collar, WS of body): Using a 3¼mm (US 3) needle, knit.

Row 2: Using a 7mm (US 10½ /11) needle, purl.

Rows 3 to 14: As rows 1 and 2, 6 times.

Row 15: Using a 4mm (US 6) needle, K3 (2: 2: 1: 1: 1), *M1, K3, rep from * to last 4 (3: 3: 2: 2: 2) sts, M1, K4 (3: 3: 2: 2: 2). 92 (98: 98: 104: 104: 104) sts.

Row 16: Using a 8mm (US 11) needle, purl.

Row 17: Using a 4mm (US 6) needle, knit.

Rows 18 to 31: As rows 16 and 17, 7 times.

Row 32: As row 16.

Row 33: Using a 4½mm (US 7) needle, knit.

Row 34: Using a 9mm (US 13) needle, purl.

Rows 35 to 40: As rows 33 and 34, 3 times.

Row 41: As row 33.

Using a 9mm (US 13) needle, cast off **loosely** knitwise (on **WS**).

Join left shoulder and collar seam, reversing seam for collar. Join side seams. Join sleeve seams. Sew sleeves into armholes.

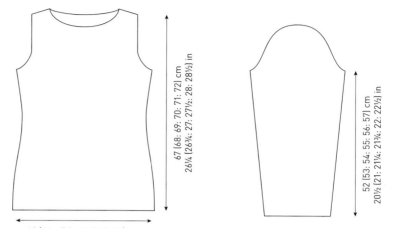

67 (68: 69: 70: 71: 72) cm
26¼ (26¾: 27: 27½: 28: 28½) in

42 (44: 47.5: 49: 52.5: 56) cm
16½ (17½: 18½: 19: 20½: 22) in

52 (53: 54: 55: 56: 57) cm
20½ (21: 21¼: 21¾: 22: 22½) in

ABLE
Close-fitting cabled skirt with shaping detail

Recommendation
Suitable for the knitter with a little experience
Please see pages 10, 11 & 35 for photographs.

	XS	S	M	L	XL	XXL	
To fit	**86**	**91**	**97**	**102**	**109**	**114**	**cm**
hips	34	36	38	40	43	45	in

Rowan Lima
	8	9	9	10	10	11	x 50gm

Photographed in Patagonia

Needles
1 pair 5mm (no 6) (US 8) needles
1 pair 5½mm (no 5) (US 9) needles
Cable needle

Extras - Waist length of 2.5 cm (1 in) wide
elastic

Tension
20 sts and 25 rows to 10 cm measured over
pattern **when slightly stretched** using 5½mm
(US 9) needles.

Special abbreviations
C4B = slip next 2 sts onto cn and leave at back
of work, K2, then K2 from cn; **C4F** = slip next
2 sts onto cn and leave at front of work, K2,
then K2 from cn; **C6B** = slip next 3 sts onto
cn and leave at back of work, K3, then K3 from
cn; **C6F** = slip next 3 sts onto cn and leave at
front of work, K3, then K3 from cn; **cn** = cable
needle.

Sizing note
Please stay true to your size as allowances
have been made within the pattern to ensure a
close-fitting garment. Also be aware that when
worn the length of the garment will be slightly
shorter than the measurement stated on the
size diagram.

BACK and FRONT (both alike)
Cast on 64 (68: 74: 78: 82: 88) sts using
5½mm (US 9) needles.
Row 1 (RS): (P4, K1, inc once in each of next
2 sts) 0 (0: 0: 0: 0: 1) times, K0 (0: 0: 3: 5: 1),
P0 (2: 5: 4: 4: 4), K4 (1: 1: 1: 1: 1), (inc once
in each of next 2 sts, K1) 0 (1: 1: 1: 1: 1) times,
(P1, K1, inc once in each of next 2 sts, K1)
twice, (P4, K1, inc once in each of next 2 sts,
K1) 4 times, P4, (K1, inc once in each of next
2 sts, K1, P1) twice, (K1, inc once in each of
next 2 sts) 0 (1: 1: 1: 1: 1) times, K4 (1: 1: 1:
1: 1), P0 (2: 5: 4: 4: 4), K0 (0: 0: 3: 5: 1), (inc
once in each of next 2 sts, K1, P4) 0 (0: 0: 0:
0: 1) times. 80 (88: 94: 98: 102: 112) sts.
Row 2: K0 (0: 0: 0: 0: 4), P0 (0: 0: 3: 5: 6),
K0 (2: 5: 4: 4: 4), P4 (6: 6: 6: 6: 6), (K1, P6)
twice, (K4, P6) 4 times, K4, (P6, K1) twice,
P4 (6: 6: 6: 6: 6), K0 (2: 5: 4: 4: 4), P0 (0: 0:
3: 5: 6), K0 (0: 0: 0: 0: 4).
Row 3: P0 (0: 0: 0: 0: 4), K0 (0: 0: 3: 5: 6),
P0 (2: 5: 4: 4: 4), K4 (6: 6: 6: 6: 6), (P1, K6)
twice, (P4, K6) 4 times, P4, (K6, P1) twice,
K4 (6: 6: 6: 6: 6), P0 (2: 5: 4: 4: 4), K0 (0: 0:
3: 5: 6), P0 (0: 0: 0: 0: 4).
Last 2 rows form rib.
Cont in rib for a further 9 rows.
Row 13: K0 (0: 0: 3: 5: 0), (P4, C6F) 0 (0: 0:
0: 0: 1) times, P0 (2: 5: 4: 4: 4), K4 (0: 0: 0:
0: 0), (C6F) 0 (1: 1: 1: 1: 1) times, (P1, C6F)
twice, (P4, C6F) twice, (P4, C6B) twice, P4,
(C6B, P1) twice, K4 (0: 0: 0: 0: 0), (C6B) 0 (1:
1: 1: 1: 1) times, P0 (2: 5: 4: 4: 4), K0 (0: 0:
3: 5: 0), (C6B, P4) 0 (0: 0: 0: 0: 1) times.
Work 1 row in rib as now set, ending with a WS row.
Last 12 rows set the sts - rib with cables
worked on every 12th row.
(Inc sts are worked within the rev st st sections
between the cables.)
Keeping sts correct as now set, work 6 rows,
ending with a WS row.
Counting in from both ends of last row,
place marker after 4th (8th: 11th: 13th:
15th: 20th) and 11th (15th: 18th: 20th:
22nd: 27th) sts - 4 markers in total.
Row 21 (RS): (Rib to marker, slip marker
to right needle, M1) twice, (rib to marker,
M1, slip marker onto right needle) twice,
rib to end.
84 (92: 98: 102: 106: 116) sts.

Work 19 rows.
Rep last 20 rows once more, and then row
21 again.
92 (100: 106: 110: 114: 124) sts.
Remove markers.
Cont straight until work measures approx
64 (65: 66: 67: 68: 69) cm, ending 5 rows
after a cable row and with a WS row.
Shape for waistband
Next row (RS): Rib 5 (9: 2: 4: 6: 1), P2tog,
*rib 8, P2tog, rep from * to last 5 (9: 2: 4: 6: 1)
sts, rib to end.
83 (91: 95: 99: 103: 111) sts.
Keeping rib correct as now set (with 3 sts
between each cable instead of 4), work 5 rows,
ending with a WS row.

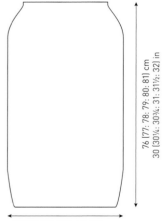

76 [77: 78: 79: 80: 81] cm
30 [30¼: 30¾: 31: 31½: 32] in

32 [34: 37: 39.5: 42: 46] cm
12½ [13½: 14½: 15½: 16½: 18] in

Continued on next page...

DEEP

Cabled hat with double turn back

Recommendation
Suitable for the knitter with a little experience
Please see page 32 for photograph.

One size

Rowan Lima
3   x 50gm
Photographed in Patagonia

Needles
1 pair 4mm (no 8) (US 6) needles
1 pair 5mm (no 6) (US 8) needles
Cable needle

Tension
20 sts and 26 rows to 10 cm measured over
pattern **when slightly stretched** using 5mm
(US 8) needles.

Special abbreviation
C4B = slip next 2 sts onto cable needle and
leave at back of work, K2, then K2 from cable
needle.

HAT
Cast on 107 sts using 4mm (US 6) needles.
Row 1 (RS): P2, *K4, P3, rep from * to end.
Row 2: *K3, P4, rep from * to last 2 sts, K2.
Rows 3 to 16: As rows 1 and 2, 7 times.
Row 17: As row 1.
Row 18: K3, *P4, K1, inc in next st, K1,
rep from * to last 6 sts, P4, K2. 121 sts.
Change to 5mm (US 8) needles.
Row 19: P2, *K4, P4, rep from * to last
7 sts, K4, P3.
Row 20: K3, *P4, K4, rep from * to last
6 sts, P4, K2.
Row 21: P2, *C4B, P4, rep from * to last
7 sts, C4B, P3.
Row 22: As row 20.
Rows 23 to 46: As rows 19 to 22, 6 times.
Rows 47 and 48: As rows 19 and 20.
Change to 4mm (US 6) needles.
Row 49: P2, *K4, P1, P2tog, P1, rep from *
to last 7 sts, K4, P3. 107 sts.
Row 50: As row 2.
Rows 51 to 56: As rows 1 and 2, 3 times.
These 56 rows complete turn-back.
Place markers at both ends of last row.
Now work main section, reversing RS of work,
as folls:
**Next row (RS of turn-back, WS of main
section):** K2, *P4, K3, rep from * to end.
Next row (RS of main section): *P3, K4, rep
from * to last 2 sts, P2.
Next row: K2, *P4, K3, rep from * to end.
Rep last 2 rows 3 times more
Change to 5mm (US 8) needles.
Now work in cable patt for main section as folls:

Row 1 (RS): *P3, K4, rep from * to last 2 sts,
P2.
Row 2: K2, *P4, K3, rep from * to end.
Rows 3 and 4: As rows 1 and 2.
Row 5: *P3, C4B, rep from * to last 2 sts, P2.
Row 6: As row 2.
Rows 7 and 8: As rows 1 and 2.
These 8 rows form cable patt for main section.
Work in patt for a further 22 rows, ending after
patt row 6 and with a WS row.
Shape top
Row 1 (RS): *P1, P2tog, K4, rep from * to last
2 sts, P2. 92 sts.
Now working 2 sts, instead of 3 sts, between
each cable, work 7 rows, ending with a WS row.
Row 9: P2tog, *K4, P2tog, rep from * to end.
76 sts.
Now working 1 st, instead of 2 sts, between
each cable, work 3 rows, ending 5 rows after
last cable row and with a WS row.
Row 13: P1, *slip next 2 sts onto cable needle
and leave at back of work, K2tog, then K2tog
from cable needle, P1, rep from * to end.
46 sts.
Keeping sts correct as now set, work 3 rows,
ending with a WS row.
Row 17: P1, *P2tog, P1, rep from * to end.
31 sts.
Row 18: K1, (K2tog) 15 times.
Break yarn and thread through rem 16 sts.
Pull up tight and fasten off securely.
Join back seam, reversing seam below
markers.
Fold turn-back to RS as in photograph, folding
cast-on edge inside turn-back.

ABLE – Continued from previous page.

Next row: Rib 7 (2: 4: 6: 8: 3), (slip next 3 sts
onto cn and leave at front of work, K2tog, K1,
then K1, K2tog from cn, P3) 4 (5: 5: 5: 5: 6)
times, (slip next 3 sts onto cn and leave at back
of work, K2tog, K1, then K1, K2tog from cn, P3)
3 (4: 4: 4: 4: 5) times, slip next 3 sts onto cn
and leave at back of work, K2tog, K1, then K1,
K2tog from cn, rib to end.
67 (71: 75: 79: 83: 87) sts.

Now working C4B instead of C6B, C4F
instead of C6F, and working cables on
every 10th row instead of every 12th row,
cont as folls:
Work 7 rows, ending with a WS row.
Change to 5mm (US 8) needles.
Work a further 16 rows, ending with
a WS row.
Cast off **loosely** in patt.

MAKING UP
Do NOT press.
Join side seams using back stitch or mattress
stitch if preferred.
Join ends of elastic to form a loop.
Lay elastic over inside of upper edge
of skirt and secure in place by working
herringbone st over elastic (to form a
casing).

Recommendation

Suitable for the knitter with a little experience
Please see pages 12 & 13 for photographs.

	XS	S	M	L	XL	XXL	
To fit	81	86	91	97	102	109	cm
bust	32	34	36	38	40	43	in

Rowan Kidsilk Haze and Fine Lace

A Kidsilk Haze

| | 5 | 5 | 6 | 6 | 7 | 7 | x 25gm |

B Fine Lace

| | 1 | 1 | 1 | 1 | 1 | 1 | x 50gm |

Photographed in Kidsilk Haze in Ghost and
Fine Lace in Cobweb

Needles

1 pair 2¾mm (no 12) (US 2) needles
1 pair 3mm (no 11) (US 2/3) needles
1 pair 4mm (no 8) (US 6) needles

Tension

21 sts and 29 rows to 10 cm measured over
stocking stitch using 4mm (US 6) needles
using only Kidsilk Haze.

Special note

We found it preferable to knit the two yarns
together from separate balls rather than
winding them together.

GLANCE
Sheer sweater with snug ribs

BACK

Cast on 106 (114: 122: 126: 134: 142) sts
using 3mm (US 2/3) needles and one strand
each of yarns A and B held together.
Row 1 (RS): K2, *P2, K2, rep from * to end.
Row 2: P2, *K2, P2, rep from * to end.
These 2 rows form rib.
Cont in rib until work measures 9 cm, ending
with a **RS** row.
Change to 4mm (US 6) needles.
Next row (WS): P0 (3: 0: 2: 9: 3), P2tog, *P6
(5: 5: 5: 4: 5), P2tog, rep from * 12 (14: 16:
16: 18: 18) times more, P0 (4: 1: 3: 9: 4).
92 (98: 104: 108: 114: 122) sts.
Break off yarn B and cont using yarn A **only**.
Beg with a K row, work in st st until back
measures 40 (40: 40: 41: 41: 41) cm, ending
with a WS row.

Shape raglan armholes

Cast off 5 sts at beg of next 2 rows.
82 (88: 94: 98: 104: 112) sts.
Work 2 rows, ending with a WS row.
Next row (RS): K3, K2tog, K to last 5 sts,
K2tog tbl, K3.
Working all decreases as set by last row,
dec 1 st at each end of 4th and 9 (8: 6:
6: 4: 1) foll 4th rows, then on foll 5 (8: 13:
14: 19: 26) alt rows.
50 (52: 52: 54: 54: 54) sts.
Work 1 row, ending with a WS row.
Cast off **loosely**.

FRONT

Work as given for back until 66 (70: 72: 76:
76: 76) sts rem in raglan armhole shaping.
Work 3 (1: 1: 1: 1: 1) rows, ending with a
WS row.

Shape front neck

Next row (RS): (K3, K2tog) 1 (0: 1: 1: 1: 1)
times, K11 (17: 13: 15: 15: 15) and turn,
leaving rem sts on a holder.
Work each side of neck separately.
Dec 1 st at neck edge of next 8 rows, then
on foll 0 (0: 0: 1: 1: 1) alt row **and at same
time** dec 1 st at raglan armhole edge of
4th (2nd: 2nd: 2nd: 2nd: 2nd) and 1 (0: 0:
0: 0: 0) foll 4th row, then on foll 0 (3: 3: 4:
4: 4) alt rows.
5 sts.
Work 1 row, ending with a WS row.

Next row (RS): K2, sl 1, K2tog, psso. 3 sts.
Next row: P3.
Next row: Sl 1, K2tog, psso.
Next row: P1 and fasten off.
With RS facing, rejoin yarn to rem sts, cast off
centre 34 (36: 36: 36: 36: 36) sts loosely, K to
last 5 (0: 5: 5: 5: 5) sts, (K2tog tbl, K3) 1 (0: 1:
1: 1: 1) times.
15 (17: 17: 19: 19: 19) sts.
Dec 1 st at neck edge of next 8 rows, then on
foll 0 (0: 0: 1: 1: 1) alt row **and at same time**
dec 1 st at raglan armhole edge of 4th (2nd:
2nd: 2nd: 2nd: 2nd) and 1 (0: 0: 0: 0: 0) foll
4th row, then on foll 0 (3: 3: 4: 4: 4) alt rows.
5 sts.
Work 1 row, ending with a WS row.
Next row (RS): K3tog, K2.
3 sts.
Next row: P3.
Next row: K3tog.
Next row: P1 and fasten off.

SLEEVES (both alike)

Cast on 50 (52: 54: 56: 58: 60) sts using 3mm
(US 2/3) needles and one strand each of yarns
A and B held together.
Row 1 (RS): P0 (1: 0: 1: 0: 1), K2, *P2, K2,
rep from * to last 0 (1: 0: 1: 0: 1) st, P0 (1: 0:
1: 0: 1).
Row 2: K0 (1: 0: 1: 0: 1), P2, *K2, P2, rep from
* to last 0 (1: 0: 1: 0: 1) st, K0 (1: 0: 1: 0: 1).
These 2 rows form rib.
Work in rib for a further 34 rows, ending with
a WS row.
Inc 1 st at each end of next row.
52 (54: 56: 58: 60: 62) sts.
Cont in rib until work measures 15 cm, ending
with a WS row.
Change to 4mm (US 6) needles.
Break off yarn B and cont using yarn A **only**.
Beg with a K row, work in st st for 6 (8: 8:
8: 8: 8) rows, ending with a WS row.
Next row (RS): K3, M1, K to last 3 sts, M1, K3.
Working all increases as set by last row, inc
1 st at each end of 10th and 7 (7: 6: 4: 3: 1)
foll 10th rows, then on 0 (0: 1: 3: 4: 6) foll
12th rows.
70 (72: 74: 76: 78: 80) sts.
Cont straight until sleeve measures 49 (50: 51:
52: 53: 54) cm, ending with a WS row.

Shape raglan

Cast off 5 sts at beg of next 2 rows.
60 (62: 64: 66: 68: 70) sts.
Working all raglan decreases in same way as
back raglan armhole decreases, dec 1 st at
each end of 3rd and 7 foll 4th rows, then on
every foll alt row until 28 sts rem.
Work 1 row, ending with RS facing for next row.

Left sleeve only

Dec 1 st at each end of next row, then cast off
6 sts at beg of foll row. 20 sts.
Dec 1 st at beg of next row, then cast off 6 sts
at beg of foll row. 13 sts.

Right sleeve only

Cast off 7 sts at beg and dec 1 st at end of next
row. 20 sts.
Work 1 row.
Cast off 6 sts at beg and dec 1 st at end of next
row. 13 sts.
Work 1 row.

Both sleeves

Rep last 2 rows once more.
Cast off rem 6 sts.

MAKING UP

Press all pieces with a warm iron over a damp
cloth.
Join both front and right back raglan seams
using back stitch or mattress stitch if preferred.

Neckband

With RS facing, using 2¾mm (US 2) needles
and yarn A, pick up and knit 24 sts from top
of left sleeve, 14 (14: 14: 15: 17: 17) sts down
left side of neck, 34 (36: 36: 36: 36: 36) sts
from front, 14 (14: 14: 15: 17: 17) sts up right
side of neck, 24 sts from top of right sleeve,
then 48 (50: 50: 52: 52: 52) sts from back.
158 (162: 162: 166: 170: 170) sts.
Beg with row 1, work in rib as given for back
for 10 rows, ending with a **RS** row.
Cast off **very loosely** in rib (on **WS**).
Join left back raglan and neckband seam.
Join side and sleeve seams.

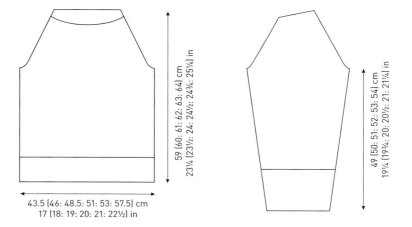

43.5 (46: 48.5: 51: 53: 57.5) cm
17 (18: 19: 20: 21: 22½) in

59 (60: 61: 62: 63: 64) cm
23¼ (23½: 24: 24½: 24¾: 25¼) in

49 (50: 51: 52: 53: 54) cm
19¼ (19¾: 20: 20½: 21: 21¼) in

Recommendation

Suitable for the knitter with a little experience
Please see pages 14 & 15 for photographs.

	XS	S	M	L	XL	XXL	
To fit	81	86	91	97	102	109	cm
bust	32	34	36	38	40	43	in

Rowan Drift

| | 7 | 7 | 8 | 8 | 9 | 10 x 100gm |

Photographed in Shore

Needles

1 pair 8mm (no 0) (US 11) needles
1 pair 10mm (no 000) (US 15) needles

Tension

10 sts and 15 rows to 10 cm measured over
pattern using 10mm (US 15) needles.

KENT
Ribbed jacket with deep raglans

BACK

Cast on 47 (49: 51: 55: 57: 61) sts using
10mm (US 15) needles.
Row 1 (RS): K3 (0: 3: 3: 0: 0), *P1, K3, rep
from * to last 0 (1: 0: 0: 1: 1) st, P0 (1: 0:
0: 1: 1).
Row 2: K1 (2: 1: 1: 2: 2), *P1, K3, rep from
* to last 2 (3: 2: 2: 3: 3) sts, P1, K1 (2: 1:
1: 2: 2).
These 2 rows form patt.
Cont in patt until back measures 20 (20:
21: 20: 20: 21) cm, ending with a WS
row.
Shape raglan armholes
Keeping patt correct, cast off 3 (4: 3: 3: 4: 4)
sts at beg of next 2 rows.
41 (41: 45: 49: 49: 53) sts.
Work 2 (2: 2: 0: 2: 0) rows.
Sizes XS and S only
Next row (RS): P1, K3, P2tog, patt to last
6 sts, P2tog tbl, K3, P1.
Next row: K2, P1, K2, patt to last 5 sts, K2,
P1, K2.
Next row: P1, K3, P1, patt to last 5 sts, P1,
K3, P1.
Next row: K2, P1, K2, patt to last 5 sts, K2,
P1, K2.
Rep last 4 rows 0 (1: -: -: -: -) times more.
39 (37: -: -: -: -) sts.
Size XXL only
Next row (RS): P1, K3, P2tog, patt to last
6 sts, P2tog tbl, K3, P1.
Next row: K2, P1, K1, K2tog tbl, patt to last
6 sts, K2tog, K1, P1, K2. 49 sts.
All sizes
Next row (RS): P1, K3, P2tog, patt to last
6 sts, P2tog tbl, K3, P1.
Next row: K2, P1, K2, patt to last 5 sts, K2,
P1, K2.
Rep last 2 rows 13 (12: 16: 18: 18: 18) times
more, ending with a WS row.
Cast off rem 11 sts.

LEFT FRONT

Cast on 25 (26: 29: 29: 30: 34) sts using
10mm (US 15) needles.
Row 1 (RS): K3 (0: 3: 3: 0: 0), *P1, K3, rep
from * to last 2 sts, K2.
Row 2: K3, *P1, K3, rep from * to last 2 (3:
2: 3: 3) sts, P1, K1 (2: 1: 1: 2: 2).

These 2 rows set the sts - front opening edge
3 sts in g st with all other sts in patt as given
for back.
Cont in patt until left front matches back to
start of raglan armhole shaping, ending with
a WS row.
Shape raglan armhole
Keeping patt correct, cast off 3 (4: 3: 3: 4: 4) sts
at beg of next row. 22 (22: 26: 26: 26: 30) sts.
Work 3 (3: 1: 1: 3: 1) rows.
Sizes XS and S only
Next row (RS): P1, K3, P2tog, patt to end.
Next row: Patt to last 5 sts, K2, P1, K2.
Next row: P1, K3, P1, patt to end.
Next row: Patt to last 5 sts, K2, P1, K2.
Rep last 4 rows 0 (1: -: -: -: -) times more.
21 (20: -: -: -: -) sts.
Sizes M and XXL only
Next row (RS): P1, K3, P2tog, patt to end.
Next row: Patt to last 6 sts, K2tog, K1, P1, K2.
Rep last 2 rows - (-: 0: -: -: 2) times more.
- (-: 24: -: -: 24) sts.
All sizes
Next row (RS): P1, K3, P2tog, patt to end.
Next row: Patt to last 5 sts, K2, P1, K2.
Rep last 2 rows 6 (5: 9: 11: 11: 9) times more,
ending with a WS row. 14 sts.
Next row (RS): Patt to last 7 sts, P2tog,
patt 5 sts.
Next row: K3, P1, K2, patt to end.
Rep last 2 rows 3 times more. 10 sts.
Next row (RS): K2tog, patt to end. 9 sts.
Cont in patt on these 9 sts only for a further
21 rows (for back neck border extension),
ending with a WS row.
Cast off.

RIGHT FRONT

Cast on 25 (26: 29: 29: 30: 34) sts using
10mm (US 15) needles.
Row 1 (RS): K2, *K3, P1, rep from * to last
3 (0: 3: 3: 0: 0) sts, K3 (0: 3: 3: 0: 0).
Row 2: K1 (2: 1: 1: 2: 2), *P1, K3, rep from
* to end.
These 2 rows set the sts - front opening
edge 3 sts in g st with all other sts in patt
as given for back.
Complete to match left front, reversing
shapings.
Cast off.

SLEEVES (both alike)

Cast on 27 (27: 29: 29: 29: 29) sts using 8mm (US 11) needles.

Row 1 (RS): P1, *K1, P1, rep from * to end.

Row 2: K1, *P1, K1, rep from * to end.

These 2 rows form rib.

Cont in rib for a further 11 rows, ending with a **RS** row.

Row 14 (WS): K1, (M1) 0 (1: 0: 0: 1: 1) times, *P1, M1, K1, M1, rep from * to last 2 sts, P1, (M1) 0 (1: 0: 0: 1: 1) times, K1.

51 (53: 55: 55: 57: 57) sts.

Change to 10mm (US 15) needles.

Starting with row 1, now work in patt as given for back until sleeve measures 32 (33: 34: 35: 36: 37) cm, ending with a WS row.

Shape raglan

Keeping patt correct, cast off 3 (4: 3: 3: 4: 4) sts at beg of next 2 rows.

45 (45: 49: 49: 49: 49) sts.

Work 2 (2: 0: 2: 2: 2) rows.

Working all raglan decreases in same way as raglan armhole decreases, dec 1 st at each end of next and 0 (1: 0: 0: 1: 1) foll 4th row, then on every foll alt row until 17 sts rem.

Work 1 row, ending with a WS row.

Left sleeve only

Dec 1 st at each end of next row, then cast off 4 sts at beg of foll row. 11 sts.

Dec 1 st at beg of next row, then cast off 5 sts at beg of foll row.

Right sleeve only

Cast off 5 sts at beg and dec 1 st at end of next row. 11 sts.

Work 1 row.

Cast off 6 sts at beg of next row.

Work 1 row.

Both sleeves

Cast off rem 5 sts.

MAKING UP

Press all pieces with a warm iron over a damp cloth.

Join all raglan seams using back stitch or mattress stitch if preferred. Join cast-off edges of back neck border extensions, then sew one edge to back neck. Join side and sleeve seams.

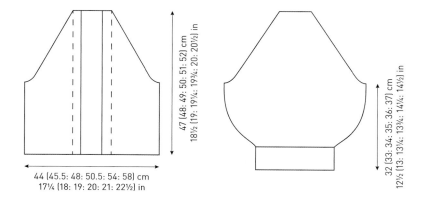

47 (48: 49: 50: 51: 52) cm
18½ (19: 19¼: 19¾: 20: 20½) in

44 (45.5: 48: 50.5: 54: 58) cm
17¼ (18: 19: 20: 21: 22½) in

32 (33: 34: 35: 36: 37) cm
12½ (13: 13¼: 13¾: 14¼: 14½) in

LOGAN
Close-fitting dress

Recommendation
Suitable for the knitter with a little experience
Please see pages 16, 17 & 33 for photographs.

	XS	S	M	L	XL	XXL	
To fit	**81**	**86**	**91**	**97**	**102**	**109**	**cm**
bust	32	34	36	38	40	43	in

Rowan Lima
| | 11 | 12 | 14 | 14 | 15 | 16 | x 50gm |

Photographed in Patagonia

Needles
1 pair 4½mm (no 7) (US 7) needles
1 pair 5mm (no 6) (US 8) needles
1 pair 5½mm (no 5) (US 9) needles
Cable needle

Tension
20 sts and 25 rows to 10 cm measured over pattern **when slightly stretched** using 5½mm (US 9) needles.

Special abbreviations
C6F = slip next 3 sts onto cable needle and leave at front of work, K3, then K3 from cable needle; **C6B** = slip next 3 sts onto cable needle and leave at back of work, K3, then K3 from cable needle.

Pattern note
When casting off across top of cables, dec 2 sts for each cable (by working K2tog twice) to avoid edges stretching out of shape.

Sizing note
Please stay true to your size as allowances have been made within the pattern to ensure a close-fitting garment. Also be aware that when worn the length of the garment will be slightly shorter than the measurement stated on the size diagram.

BACK
Cast on 76 (80: 86: 90: 92: 100) sts using 5mm (US 8) needles.
Row 1 (RS): P2 (4: 7: 9: 3: 7), (K1, inc once in each of next 2 sts, K1, P3) 0 (0: 0: 0: 1: 1) times, K1, inc once in each of next 2 sts, K1, (P3, K1, inc once in each of next 2 sts, K1) twice, (P4, K1, inc once in each of next 2 sts, K1) 4 times, P4, (K1, inc once in each of next 2 sts, K1, P3) twice, K1, inc once in each of next 2 sts, K1, (P3, K1, inc once in each of next 2 sts, K1) 0 (0: 0: 0: 1: 1) times, P2 (4: 7: 9: 3: 7).
96 (100: 106: 110: 116: 124) sts.
Row 2: K2 (4: 7: 9: 3: 7), P6, (K3, P6) 2 (2: 2: 2: 3: 3) times, (K4, P6) 4 times, K4, (P6, K3) 2 (2: 2: 2: 3: 3) times, P6, K2 (4: 7: 9: 3: 7).
Row 3: P2 (4: 7: 9: 3: 7), K6, (P3, K6) 2 (2: 2: 2: 3: 3) times, (P4, K6) 4 times, P4, (K6, P3) 2 (2: 2: 2: 3: 3) times, K6, P2 (4: 7: 9: 3: 7).
Last 2 rows form rib.
Cont in rib for a further 7 rows.
Change to 5½mm (US 9) needles.
Counting in from both ends of last row, place marker after 1st (3rd: 6th: 8th: 11th: 15th) st, (miss next 9 sts and place another marker after 9th st) twice - 6 markers in total.
Row 11 (RS): (Rib to marker, M1, slip marker to right needle) 3 times, (rib to marker, slip marker onto right needle, M1) 3 times, rib to end.
102 (106: 112: 116: 122: 130) sts.
Working inc sts as K sts on next row, work 1 row.
Row 13: P3 (5: 8: 10: 3: 7), C6F, (P4, C6F) 4 (4: 4: 4: 5: 5) times, P4, (C6B, P4) 4 (4: 4: 4: 5: 5) times, C6B, P3 (5: 8: 10: 3: 7).
Work 1 row in rib as now set, ending with a WS row.
Last 12 rows set the sts - rib with cables worked on every 12th row. (Inc and dec sts are worked within the rev st st sections between the cables.)
Keeping sts correct as now set, work 6 rows, ending with a WS row.
Row 21: As row 11.
108 (112: 118: 122: 128: 136) sts.

Remove outer markers, leaving 4 markers in total.
Work 23 rows, ending with a WS row.
Row 45 (RS): P2tog, (patt to within 2 sts of marker, P2tog, slip marker onto right needle) twice, (patt to marker, slip marker onto right needle, P2tog tbl) twice, patt to last 2 sts, P2tog tbl.
102 (106: 112: 116: 122: 130) sts.
Work 17 rows.
Rep last 18 rows once more, then row 45 again.
90 (94: 100: 104: 110: 118) sts.
Work 33 rows, ending with a WS row.
Row 115 (RS): Inc in first st, (patt to within 1 st of marker, inc in next st, slip marker onto right needle) twice, (patt to marker, slip marker onto right needle, inc in next st) twice, patt to last st, inc in last st.
96 (100: 106: 110: 116: 124) sts.
Work 15 rows.
Row 131: As row 115.
102 (106: 112: 116: 122: 130) sts.
Remove markers.
Cont straight until back measures 60 (60: 60: 61: 61: 61) cm, ending with a WS row.
Shape armholes
Keeping patt correct, cast off 3 (4: 4: 5: 5: 6) sts at beg of next 2 rows.
96 (98: 104: 106: 112: 118) sts.
Dec 1 st at each end of next 5 (5: 7: 7: 9: 9) rows, then on foll 3 (3: 3: 3: 3: 4) alt rows, then on foll 4th row.
78 (80: 82: 84: 86: 90) sts.
Cont straight until armhole measures 18 (19: 20: 20: 21: 22) cm, ending with a WS row.
Shape shoulders and back neck
Cast off 6 (6: 7: 7: 7: 8) sts at beg of next 2 rows. 66 (68: 68: 70: 72: 74) sts.
Next row (RS): Cast off 6 (6: 7: 7: 7: 8) sts, patt until there are 11 (11: 10: 10: 11: 11) sts on right needle and turn, leaving rem sts on a holder.
Work each side of neck separately.
Cast off 4 sts at beg of next row.
Cast off rem 7 (7: 6: 6: 7: 7) sts.
With RS facing, rejoin yarn to rem sts, cast off centre 32 (34: 34: 36: 36: 36) sts, patt to end.
Complete to match first side, reversing shapings.

FRONT

Work as given for back until 20 (20: 20: 22: 22: 22) rows less have been worked than on back to start of shoulder shaping, ending with a WS row.

Shape front neck

Next row (RS): Patt 29 (29: 30: 31: 32: 34) sts and turn, leaving rem sts on a holder.
Work each side of neck separately.
Keeping patt correct, dec 1 st at neck edge of next 6 rows, then on foll 3 (3: 3: 4: 4: 4) alt rows, then on foll 4th row.
19 (19: 20: 20: 21: 23) sts.
Work 3 rows, ending with a WS row.

Shape shoulder

Cast off 6 (6: 7: 7: 7: 8) sts at beg of next and foll alt row.
Work 1 row.
Cast off rem 7 (7: 6: 6: 7: 7) sts.
With RS facing, rejoin yarn to rem sts, cast off centre 20 (22: 22: 22: 22: 22) sts, patt to end.
Complete to match first side, reversing shapings.

LEFT SLEEVE

Cast on 38 (40: 42: 44: 46: 48) sts using 5mm (US 8) needles.
Row 1 (RS): P1 (2: 3: 4: 5: 6), (K1, inc once in each of next 2 sts, K1, P4) 4 times, K1, inc once in each of next 2 sts, K1, P1 (2: 3: 4: 5: 6).
48 (50: 52: 54: 56: 58) sts.
Row 2: K1 (2: 3: 4: 5: 6), P6, (K4, P6) 4 times, K1 (2: 3: 4: 5: 6).
Row 3: P1 (2: 3: 4: 5: 6), K6, (P4, K6) 4 times, P1 (2: 3: 4: 5: 6).
Last 2 rows form rib.
Cont in rib for a further 7 rows.
Change to 5½mm (US 9) needles.
Cont in rib for a further 4 (6: 8: 8: 0: 2) rows, ending with a WS row.
Next row (RS): Inc in first st, P0 (1: 2: 3: 4: 5), C6F, (P4, C6F) 4 times, P0 (1: 2: 3: 4: 5), inc in last st.
50 (52: 54: 56: 58: 60) sts.
Last 12 rows set the sts - rib with cables worked on every 12th row - and beg sleeve shaping.
Keeping sts correct as now set, work in patt, shaping sides by inc 1 st at each end of 10th and 8 (8: 8: 7: 1: 1) foll 10th rows, then on – (–: –: 1: 7: 7) foll 12th rows.
68 (70: 72: 74: 76: 78) sts.
Cont straight until sleeve measures 46 (47: 48: 49: 50: 51) cm, ending after same patt row as on back to start of armhole shaping and with a WS row.

Shape top

Keeping patt correct, cast off 3 (4: 4: 5: 5: 6) sts at beg of next 2 rows.
62 (62: 64: 64: 66: 66) sts.
Dec 1 st at each end of next 3 rows, then on foll alt row, then on 4 foll 4th rows.
46 (46: 48: 48: 50: 50) sts.
Work 1 row.
Dec 1 st at each end of next and foll 1 (3: 4: 4: 5: 7) alt rows, then on foll 7 (5: 5: 5: 5: 3) rows, ending with a WS row.
Cast off rem 28 sts.

RIGHT SLEEVE

Work as given for left sleeve, replacing "C6F" with "C6B".

MAKING UP

Do NOT press.
Join right shoulder seam using back stitch or mattress stitch if preferred.

Neckband

With RS facing and using 4½mm (US 7) needles, pick up and knit 23 (23: 23: 25: 25: 25) sts down left side of neck, 16 (18: 18: 18: 18: 18) sts from front, 23 (23: 23: 25: 25: 25) sts up right side of neck, then 32 (34: 34: 38: 38: 38) sts from back.
94 (98: 98: 106: 106: 106) sts.
Row 1 (WS): P2, *K2, P2, rep from * to end.
Row 2: K2, *P2, K2, rep from * to end.
Rep last 2 rows 4 times more, ending with a RS row.
Cast off in rib (on **WS**).
Join left shoulder and neckband seam.
Join side seams. Join sleeve seams.
Sew sleeves into armholes.

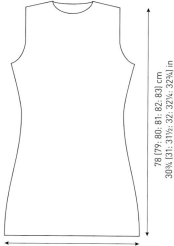

78 (79: 80: 81: 82: 83] cm
30¾ (31: 31½: 32: 32¼: 32¾) in

40.5 (43: 45.5: 48: 50.5: 54.5) cm
16 (17: 18: 19: 20: 21½) in

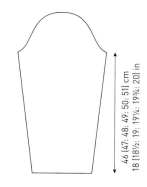

46 (47: 48: 49: 50: 51) cm
18 (18½: 19: 19¼: 19¾: 20] in

WILL

Pretty cabled cardigan worked in two ends of yarn

Recommendation

Suitable for the knitter with a little experience
Please see pages 18 & 19 for photographs.

	XS	S	M	L	XL	XXL	
To fit	81	86	91	97	102	109	cm
bust	32	34	36	38	40	43	in

Rowan Kidsilk Haze and Fine Lace

A Kidsilk Haze

| | 7 | 8 | 9 | 9 | 10 | 10 | x 25gm |

B Fine Lace

| | 3 | 4 | 4 | 4 | 5 | 5 | x 50gm |

Photographed in Kidsilk Haze in Anthracite
and Fine Lace in Gunmetal

Needles

1 pair 3mm (no 11) (US 2/3) needles
1 pair 3¾mm (no 9) (US 5) needles
Cable needle

Buttons – 7

Tension

21 sts and 30 rows to 10 cm measured over
reverse stocking stitch using 3¾mm (US 5)
needles and one strand each of Kidsilk Haze
and Fine Lace held together.

Special abbreviations

C6B = slip next 3 sts onto cn and leave at back
of work, K3, then K3 from cn; **C6F** = slip next 3
sts onto cn and leave at front of work, K3, then
K3 from cn; **cn** = cable needle.Will
Pretty cabled cardigan worked in two ends of
yarn

Special note

We found it preferable to knit the two yarns
together from separate balls rather than
winding them together.

BACK

Cast on 173 (181: 187: 195: 203: 213) sts
using 3¾mm (US 5) needles and one strand
each of yarns A and B held together.
Row 1 (RS): K0 (0: 0: 4: 0: 0), P0 (4: 7: 7: 0:
5), *K8, P7, rep from * to last 8 (12: 0: 4: 8:
13) sts, K8 (8: 0: 4: 8: 8), P0 (4: 0: 0: 0: 5).
Row 2: P0 (0: 0: 4: 0: 0), K0 (4: 7: 7: 0: 5),
*P8, K7, rep from * to last 8 (12: 0: 4: 8: 13)
sts, P8 (8: 0: 4: 8: 8), K0 (4: 0: 0: 0: 5).
These 2 rows form rib.
Cont in rib until work measures 16 cm, ending
with a **RS** row.
Next row (WS): (P2, P2tog) 0 (0: 0: 1: 0: 0)
times, (K2tog) 0 (0: 0: 1: 0: 0) times, K0 (2:
5: 3: 0: 3), (K2tog tbl) 0 (1: 1: 1: 0: 1) times,
*P2tog tbl, P4, P2tog, K2tog, K3, K2tog tbl, rep
from * to last 8 (12: 15: 4: 8: 13) sts, P2tog
tbl, P4 (4: 4: 2: 4: 4), (P2tog) 1 (1: 1: 0: 1: 1)
times, (K2tog) 0 (1: 1: 0: 0: 1) times, K0 (2: 5:
0: 0: 3). 127 (133: 139: 143: 149: 157) sts.
Now work in patt as folls:
Row 1 (RS): P0 (3: 6: 3: 0: 4), K6 (0: 0: 0: 6:
0), (C6B) 0 (1: 1: 0: 0: 1) times, (P5, C6B) 5 (5:
5: 6: 6: 6) times, P5, (C6F, P5) 5 (5: 5: 6: 6: 6)
times, (C6F) 0 (1: 1: 0: 0: 1) times, K6 (0: 0: 0:
6: 0), P0 (3: 6: 3: 0: 4).
Row 2: P0 (0: 0: 3: 0: 0), K0 (3: 6: 5: 0: 4),
*P6, K5, rep from * to last 6 (9: 1: 3: 6: 10) sts,
P6 (6: 0: 3: 6: 6), K0 (3: 1: 0: 0: 4).
Row 3: K0 (0: 0: 3: 0: 0), P0 (3: 6: 5: 0: 4),
*K6, P5, rep from * to last 6 (9: 1: 3: 6: 10) sts,
K6 (6: 0: 3: 6: 6), P0 (3: 1: 0: 0: 4).
Rows 4 to 9: As rows 2 and 3, 3 times.
Row 10: As row 2.
These 10 rows form patt.
Cont in patt until back measures 35 (35: 35:
36: 36: 36) cm, ending with a WS row.

Shape armholes

Keeping patt correct, cast off 5 (5: 5: 6: 6: 6)
sts at beg of next 2 rows. 117 (123: 129: 131:
137: 145) sts.
Dec 1 st at each end of next 7 (9: 11: 11: 13:
15) rows, then on foll 5 alt rows, then on foll
4th row. 91 (93: 95: 97: 99: 103) sts.
Cont straight until armhole measures 18 (19:
20: 20: 21: 22) cm, ending with a WS row.

Shape shoulders and back neck

Cast off 8 (8: 8: 8: 9: 9) sts at beg of next
2 rows. 75 (77: 79: 81: 81: 85) sts.

Next row (RS): Cast off 8 (8: 8: 8: 9: 9) sts,
patt until there are 12 (12: 13: 13: 12: 14)
sts on right needle and turn, leaving rem sts
on a holder.
Work each side of neck separately.
Cast off 4 sts at beg of next row.
Cast off rem 8 (8: 9: 9: 8: 10) sts.
With RS facing, rejoin yarns to rem sts,
cast off centre 35 (37: 37: 39: 39: 39)
sts, patt to end.
Complete to match first side, rev shapings.

LEFT FRONT

Cast on 94 (98: 101: 105: 109: 114) sts using
3¾mm (US 5) needles and one strand each of
yarns A and B held together.
Row 1 (RS): K0 (0: 0: 4: 0: 0), P0 (4: 7: 7: 0: 5),
*K8, P7, rep from * to last 19 sts, K8, P5, K6.
Row 2: K11, *P8, K7, rep from * to last 8 (12: 0:
4: 8: 13) sts, P8 (8: 0: 4: 8: 8), K0 (4: 0: 0: 0: 5).
These 2 rows set the sts - front opening edge
6 sts in g st with all other sts in rib.
Cont as set until work measures 16 cm, ending
with a **RS** row.
Next row (WS): K9, K2tog tbl, *P2tog tbl, P4,
P2tog, K2tog, K3, K2tog tbl, rep from * to last
8 (12: 15: 4: 8: 13) sts, P2tog tbl, P4 (4: 4: 2:
4: 4), (P2tog) 1 (1: 1: 0: 1: 1) times, (K2tog)
0 (1: 1: 0: 0: 1) times, K0 (2: 5: 0: 0: 3).
71 (74: 77: 79: 82: 86) sts.
Now work in patt as folls:
Row 1 (RS): P0 (3: 6: 3: 0: 4), K6 (0: 0: 0:
6: 0), (C6B) 0 (1: 1: 0: 0: 1) times, (P5, C6B)
5 (5: 5: 6: 6: 6) times, P4, K6.
Row 2: K10, *P6, K5, rep from * to last
6 (9: 1: 3: 6: 10) sts, P6 (6: 0: 3: 6: 6),
K0 (3: 1: 0: 0: 4).
Row 3: K0 (0: 0: 3: 0: 0), P0 (3: 6: 5: 0: 4),
*K6, P5, rep from * to last 16 sts, K6, P4, K6.
Rows 4 to 9: As rows 2 and 3, 3 times.
Row 10: As row 2.
These 10 rows set the sts - front opening edge
6 sts still in g st with all other sts now in patt
as given for back.
Cont in patt until left front matches back to start
of armhole shaping, ending with a WS row.

Shape armhole

Keeping patt correct, cast off 5 (5: 5: 6: 6: 6)
sts at beg of next row. 66 (69: 72: 73: 76: 80) sts.
Work 1 row.

Dec 1 st at armhole edge of next 7 (9: 11: 11: 13: 15) rows, then on foll 5 alt rows, then on foll 4th row. 53 (54: 55: 56: 57: 59) sts.
Cont straight until 20 (20: 20: 22: 22: 22) rows less have been worked than on back to start of shoulder shaping, ending with a WS row.

Shape neck
Next row (RS): Patt 34 (34: 35: 36: 37: 39) sts and turn, leaving rem 19 (20: 20: 20: 20: 20) sts on a holder.
Keeping patt correct, dec 1 st at neck edge of next 6 rows, then on foll 3 (3: 3: 4: 4: 4) alt rows, then on foll 4th row. 24 (24: 25: 25: 26: 28) sts.
Work 3 rows, ending with a WS row.

Shape shoulder
Cast off 8 (8: 8: 8: 9: 9) sts at beg of next and foll alt row.
Work 1 row.
Cast off rem 8 (8: 9: 9: 8: 10) sts.
Mark positions for 7 buttons along left front opening edge - first to come in patt row 1, last to come just above neck shaping, and rem 5 buttons evenly spaced between.

RIGHT FRONT
Cast on 94 (98: 101: 105: 109: 114) sts using 3¾mm (US 5) needles and one strand each of yarns A and B held together.
Row 1 (RS): K6, P5, K8, *P7, K8, rep from * to last 0 (4: 7: 11: 0: 5) sts, P0 (4: 7: 7: 0: 5), K0 (0: 0: 4: 0: 0).
Row 2: K0 (4: 0: 0: 0: 5), P8 (8: 0: 4: 8: 8), *K7, P8, rep from * to last 11 sts, K11.
These 2 rows set the sts - front opening edge 6 sts in g st with all other sts in rib.
Cont as set until work measures 16 cm, ending with a **RS** row.
Next row (WS): K0 (2: 5: 0: 0: 3), (K2tog tbl) 0 (1: 1: 0: 0: 1) times, (P2tog tbl) 1 (1: 1: 0: 1: 1) times, P4 (4: 4: 2: 4: 4), P2tog, *K2tog, K3, K2tog tbl, P2tog tbl, P4, P2tog, rep from * to last 11 sts, K2tog, K9. 71 (74: 77: 79: 82: 86) sts.
Now work in patt as folls:
Row 1 (RS): K2, K2tog tbl, yfwd (to make a buttonhole), K2, P4, (C6F, P5) 5 (5: 5: 6: 6: 6) times, (C6F) 0 (1: 1: 0: 0: 1) times, K6 (0: 0: 0: 6: 0), P0 (3: 6: 3: 0: 4).
Working a further 5 buttonholes in this way to correspond with positions marked for buttons on left front and noting that no further reference will be made to buttonholes, cont as folls:
Row 2: K0 (3: 1: 0: 0: 4), P6 (6: 0: 3: 6: 6), *K5, P6, rep from * to last 10 sts, K10.
Row 3: K6, P4, K6, *P5, K6, rep from * to last 0 (3: 6: 8: 0: 4) sts, P0 (3: 6: 5: 0: 4), K0 (0: 0: 3: 0: 0).
Rows 4 to 9: As rows 2 and 3, 3 times.

Row 10: As row 2.
These 10 rows set the sts - front opening edge 6 sts still in g st with all other sts now in patt as given for back.
Complete to match left front, rev shapings and working first row of neck shaping as folls:

Shape neck
Next row (RS): K6, P4, (K2tog) 3 times, P3 (4: 4: 4: 4: 4) and slip these 16 (17: 17: 17: 17: 17) sts onto a holder, patt to end. 34 (34: 35: 36: 37: 39) sts.

LEFT SLEEVE
Cast on 62 (64: 66: 68: 70: 72) sts using 3¾mm (US 5) needles and one strand each of yarns A and B held together.
Work in patt as folls:
Row 1 (RS): K1 (2: 3: 4: 5: 6), P5, *K6, P5, rep from * to last 1 (2: 3: 4: 5: 6) sts, K1 (2: 3: 4: 5: 6).
Row 2: P1 (2: 3: 4: 5: 6), K5, *P6, K5, rep from * to last 1 (2: 3: 4: 5: 6) sts, P1 (2: 3: 4: 5: 6).
Rows 3 to 10: As rows 1 and 2, 4 times, inc 1 st at each end of 7th of these rows. 64 (66: 68: 70: 72: 74) sts.
Row 11: (P1, C6B) 0 (0: 0: 0: 0: 1) times, K2 (3: 4: 5: 6: 0), P5, *C6B, P5, rep from * to last 2 (3: 4: 5: 6: 7) sts, K2 (3: 4: 5: 6: 0), (C6B, P1) 0 (0: 0: 0: 0: 1) times.
Row 12: K0 (0: 0: 0: 0: 1), P2 (3: 4: 5: 6: 6), K5, *P6, K5, rep from * to last 2 (3: 4: 5: 6: 7) sts, P2 (3: 4: 5: 6: 6), K0 (0: 0: 0: 0: 1).
Rows 3 to 12 **only** form patt and beg sleeve shaping.
Cont in patt, shaping sides by inc 1 st at each end of 7th and every foll 10th row to 82 (82: 80: 80: 78: 78) sts, then on every foll 12th row until there are 86 (88: 90: 92: 94: 96) sts, taking inc sts into patt.
Cont straight until sleeve measures 46 (47: 48: 49: 50: 51) cm, ending with a WS row.

Shape top
Keeping patt correct, cast off 5 (5: 5: 6: 6: 6) sts at beg of next 2 rows.
76 (78: 80: 80: 82: 84) sts.
Dec 1 st at each end of next 3 rows, then on foll 4th row, then on 5 foll 4th rows.
58 (60: 62: 62: 64: 66) sts.
Work 1 row, ending with a WS row.
Dec 1 st at each end of next and every foll alt row to 50 sts, then on foll 5 rows, ending with a WS row.
Cast off rem 40 sts.

RIGHT SLEEVE
Work as given for left sleeve, but replacing "C6B" with "C6F" throughout.

MAKING UP
Press all pieces with a warm iron over a damp cloth.
Join both shoulder seams using back stitch or mattress stitch if preferred.

Neckband
With RS facing, using 3mm (US 2/3) needles and one strand each of yarns A and B held together, slip 16 (17: 17: 17: 17: 17) sts on right front holder onto right needle, rejoin yarn and pick up and knit 20 (20: 20: 22: 22: 22) sts up right side of neck, 35 (37: 37: 39: 39: 39) sts from back, and 20 (20: 20: 22: 22: 22) sts down left side of neck, then work across 19 (20: 20: 20: 20: 20) sts on left front holder as folls: P3 (4: 4: 4: 4: 4), (K2tog) 3 times, P4, K6. 107 (111: 111: 117: 117: 117) sts.
Row 1 (WS): Knit.
Row 2: K2, K2tog tbl, yfwd (to make 7th buttonhole), K to end.
Work in g st for a further 6 rows, ending with
a **RS** row.
Cast off **loosely** knitwise (on **WS**).
Join side seams. Join sleeve seams. Sew sleeves into armholes. Sew on buttons.

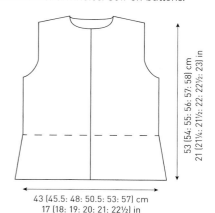

43 (45.5: 48: 50.5: 53: 57) cm
17 (18: 19: 20: 21: 22½) in

53 [54: 55: 56: 57: 58] cm
21 (21¼: 21½: 22: 22½: 23) in

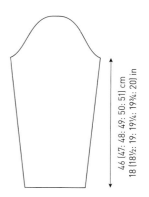

46 (47: 48: 49: 50: 51) cm
18 (18½: 19: 19¼: 19¾: 20) in

SHARP
Neat crochet jacket with pocket & epaulet detail

Recommendation
Suitable for the crocheter with a little experience
Please see pages 22, 23 & 25 for photographs.

	XS	S	M	L	XL	XXL	
To fit	**81**	**86**	**91**	**97**	**102**	**109**	**cm**
bust	32	34	36	38	40	43	in

Rowan Felted Tweed Aran

| | 14 | 15 | 16 | 16 | 17 | 18 | x 50gm |

Photographed in Soot

Crochet hooks
5.50mm (no 5) (US I9) crochet hook
6.00mm (no 4) (US J10) crochet hook

Needles
1 pair 4mm (no 8) (US 6) needles

Buttons – 13

Tension
13.5 sts and 10 rows to 10 cm measured over
pattern using 6.00mm (US J10) crochet hook.

Crochet abbreviations
ch = chain; **dc** = double crochet; **dc2tog** =
(insert hook as indicated, yoh and draw loop
through) twice, yoh and draw through all 3
loops; **ss** = slip stitch; **tr** = treble; **tr2tog** =
(yoh and insert hook as indicated, yoh and
draw loop through, yoh and draw through 2
loop) twice, yoh and draw through all 3 loop;
yoh = yarn over hook.

BACK
Lower right back
Make 34 (36: 38: 40: 42: 44) ch using
6.00mm (US J10) hook.
Foundation row (RS): 1 tr into 5th ch from
hook, 1 tr into ch **before** one just worked into
enclosing previous tr in this st, *miss next ch,
1 tr into next ch, 1 tr into missed ch enclosing
previous tr in this st, rep from * to last ch, 1 tr
into last ch, turn. 32 (34: 36: 38: 40: 42) sts.
Now work in patt as folls:
Row 1 (WS): 1 ch (does NOT count as st),
1 dc into each tr to end, working last dc into
top of 3 ch at beg of previous row, turn.
Row 2: 3 ch (counts as first tr), miss dc at
base of 3 ch, *miss next dc, 1 tr into next dc,
1 tr into missed dc enclosing previous tr in this
st, rep from * to last dc, 1 tr into last dc, turn.
These 2 rows form patt.
Cont in patt for a further 3 rows.
Row 6 (RS): 3 ch (counts as first tr), miss dc
at base of 3 ch, tr2tog over next 2 dc - 1 st
decreased, patt to end, turn.
31 (33: 35: 37: 39: 41) sts.
Row 7: 1 ch (does NOT count as st), 1 dc into
each st to end, working last dc into top of 3 ch
at beg of previous row, turn.
Row 8: 3 ch (counts as first tr), miss dc at
base of 3 ch, 1 tr into next dc, patt to end, turn.
Work 1 row.
Row 10: 3 ch (does NOT count as st), miss dc
at base of 3 ch - 1 st decreased, 1 tr into next
dc, patt to end, turn. 30 (32: 34: 36: 38: 40) sts.
Work 2 rows, ending with a **RS** row.
Break yarn.
Lower left back
Work as given for lower right back to beg of row 6.
Row 6 (RS): Patt to last 3 dc, tr2tog over next
2 dc - 1 st decreased, 1 tr into last dc, turn.
31 (33: 35: 37: 39: 41) sts.
Row 7: 1 ch (does NOT count as st), 1 dc into
each st to end, working last dc into top of 3 ch
at beg of previous row, turn.
Row 8: Patt to last 2 dc, 1 tr into each of last
2 dc, turn.
Work 1 row.
Row 10: Patt to last 2 dc, tr2tog over last
2 dc - 1 st decreased, turn.
30 (32: 34: 36: 38: 40) sts.
Work 2 rows, ending with a **RS** row.

Join sections
Row 13 (WS): Patt to last 4 sts of lower left
back, holding RS of lower left back against WS
of lower right back work 1 dc through both
next st of lower left back and first st of lower
right back, (work 1 dc through both next st of
lower left back and next st of lower right back)
3 times, patt to end of lower right back.
56 (60: 64: 68: 72: 76) sts.
Working decreases as set by side seam edges
of lower backs, dec 1 st at each end of next
and foll 4th row.
52 (56: 60: 64: 68: 72) sts.
Work 9 rows.
Row 28 (RS): 3 ch (counts as first tr), 1 tr into
dc at base of 3 ch - 1 st increased, patt to last
dc, 2 tr into last dc - 1 st increased, turn.
54 (58: 62: 66: 70: 74) sts.
Work 1 row.
Row 30: 3 ch (counts as first tr), miss dc at
base of 3 ch, 1 tr into next dc, patt to last 2 dc,
1 tr into each of last 2 dc, turn.
Work 1 row.
Row 32 (RS): 3 ch (counts as first tr), miss dc
at base of 3 ch, 1 tr into next dc, 1 tr into dc at
base of 3 ch enclosing previous tr in this st -
1 st increased, patt to last 2 dc, miss 1 dc, 1 tr
into last dc, 1 tr into dc just missed enclosing
previous tr in this st, 1 tr into last dc - 1 st
increased, turn.
56 (60: 64: 68: 72: 76) sts.
Work 7 rows, ending with a WS row.
(Back should measure 40 cm.)
Shape armholes
Next row (RS): Ss across and into 4th dc,
3 ch (counts as first tr), miss dc at base of 3
ch, 1 tr into next dc - 3 sts decreased, patt to
last 5 dc, 1 tr into each of next 2 dc and turn,
leaving rem 3 sts unworked - 3 sts decreased.
50 (54: 58: 62: 66: 70) sts.
Next row: 1 ch (does NOT count as st),
dc2tog over first 2 tr - 1 st decreased, 1 dc into
each st to last 2 sts, dc2tog over last 2 sts - 1
st decreased, turn.
48 (52: 56: 60: 64: 68) sts.
Next row: 3 ch (counts as first tr), miss dc
at base of 3 ch, tr2tog over next 2 dc - 1 st
decreased, patt to last 3 dc, tr2tog over next
2 dc - 1 st decreased, 1 tr into last dc, turn.
46 (50: 54: 58: 62: 66) sts.

Next row: 1 ch (does NOT count as st), dc2tog over first 2 tr - 1 st decreased, 1 dc into each st to last 2 sts, dc2tog over last 2 sts - 1 st decreased, turn.
44 (48: 52: 56: 60: 64) sts.
Rep last 2 rows 0 (1: 1: 2: 2: 3) times more.
44 (44: 48: 48: 52: 52) sts.
Work 11 (11: 11: 9: 11: 9) rows, ending with a **RS** row.

Shape back neck
Next row (WS): Patt first 12 (12: 14: 13: 15: 15) sts and turn, leaving rem sts unworked.
Next row: 3 ch (does NOT count as st), miss dc at base of 3 ch, 1 tr into next 0 (0: 0: 1: 1: 1) dc, patt to end, turn.
Work 1 row on these 11 (11: 13: 12: 14: 14) sts.
Fasten off.
Return to last complete row worked, miss next 20 (20: 20: 22: 22: 22) dc, attach yarn to next st and cont as folls:
Next row (WS): 1 ch (does NOT count as st), 1 dc into st at base of 1 ch, 1 dc into each st to end, turn.
12 (12: 14: 13: 15: 15) sts.
Next row: 3 ch (counts as first tr), miss dc at base of 3 ch, patt next 8 (8: 10: 8: 10: 10) sts, (1 tr into next dc) 0 (0: 0: 1: 1: 1) times, tr2tog over last 2 dc, turn.
Work 1 row on these 11 (11: 13: 12: 14: 14) sts.
Fasten off.

LOWER POCKET LININGS (make 2)
Make 18 (18: 18: 20: 20: 20) ch using 6.00mm (US J10) hook.
Work foundation row as given for back.
16 (16: 16: 18: 18: 18) sts.
Beg with row 1, work in patt as given for back for 10 rows, ending with a **RS** row.
Break yarn.

UPPER POCKET LININGS (make 2)
Make 14 (14: 14: 16: 16: 16) ch using 6.00mm (US J10) hook.
Work foundation row as given for back.
12 (12: 12: 14: 14: 14) sts.
Beg with row 1, work in patt as given for back for 6 rows, ending with a **RS** row.
Break yarn.

LEFT FRONT
Make 36 (38: 40: 42: 44: 46) ch using 6.00mm (US J10) hook.
Work foundation row as given for back.
34 (36: 38: 40: 42: 44) sts.
Now work in patt as given for back for 5 rows, ending with a WS row.

Working all decreases and increases as given for back, cont as folls:
Dec 1 st at beg of next and 2 foll 4th rows, ending with a **RS** row.
31 (33: 35: 37: 39: 41) sts.
Place lower pocket
Next row (WS): Patt 12 sts, miss next 16 (16: 16: 18: 18: 18) sts and, in their place, patt across 16 (16: 16: 18: 18: 18) sts of first lower pocket lining, patt rem 3 (5: 7: 7: 9: 11) sts, turn.
Work 2 rows.
Dec 1 st at beg of next row.
30 (32: 34: 36: 38: 40) sts.
Work 9 rows.
Inc 1 st at beg of next and foll 4th row.
32 (34: 36: 38: 40: 42) sts.
Work 6 rows, ending with a **RS** row.
Place upper pocket
Next row (WS): Patt 12 sts, miss next 12 (12: 12: 14: 14: 14) sts and, in their place, patt across 12 (12: 12: 14: 14: 14) sts of first upper pocket lining, patt rem 8 (10: 12: 12: 14: 16) sts, turn.
Shape armhole
Dec 3 sts at beg of next row.
29 (31: 33: 35: 37: 39) sts.
Dec 1 st at armhole edge of next 3 (5: 5: 7: 7: 9) rows.
26 (26: 28: 28: 30: 30) sts.
Cont straight until 7 rows less have been worked than on back to shoulder fasten-off, ending with a **RS** row.
Break yarn.
Shape neck
Next row (WS): Miss first 11 (11: 11: 12: 12: 12) sts, attach yarn to next st, 1 ch (does NOT count as st), 1 dc into st at base of 1 ch, patt to end, turn.
15 (15: 17: 16: 18: 18) sts.
Dec 1 st at neck edge of next 4 rows.
11 (11: 13: 12: 14: 14) sts.
Work a further 2 rows, ending with a WS row.
Fasten off.

RIGHT FRONT
Make 36 (38: 40: 42: 44: 46) ch using 6.00mm (US J10) hook.
Work foundation row as given for back.
34 (36: 38: 40: 42: 44) sts.
Now work in patt as given for back for 5 rows, ending with a WS row.
Working all decreases and increases as given for back, cont as folls:
Dec 1 st at end of next and 2 foll 4th rows, ending with a **RS** row.
31 (33: 35: 37: 39: 41) sts.

Place lower pocket
Next row (WS): Patt 3 (5: 7: 7: 9: 11) sts, miss next 16 (16: 16: 18: 18: 18) sts and, in their place, patt across 16 (16: 16: 18: 18: 18) sts of second lower pocket lining, patt rem 12 sts, turn.
Complete to match left front, reversing shapings and working first row of neck shaping as folls:
Shape neck
Next row (WS): Patt to last 11 (11: 11: 12: 12: 12) sts and turn, leaving rem sts unworked. 15 (15: 17: 16: 18: 18) sts.

SLEEVES (both alike)
Make 30 (32: 32: 34: 36: 36) ch using 6.00mm (US J10) hook.
Work foundation row as given for back.
28 (30: 30: 32: 34: 34) sts.
Now work in patt as given for back for 3 rows, ending with a WS row.
Working all decreases and increases as given for back, cont as folls:
Inc 1 st at each end of next and 1 (0: 0: 0: 0: 0) foll 4th row, then on 5 (6: 6: 2: 2: 1) foll 6th rows, then on 0 (0: 0: 3: 0: 4) foll 8th rows.
42 (44: 44: 44: 46: 46) sts.
Work 5 (5: 5: 7: 7: 7) rows, ending with a WS row.
Shape top
Working all decreases as set by back armhole, dec 3 sts at each end of next row.
36 (38: 38: 38: 40: 40) sts.
Dec 1 st at each end of next 12 (13: 13: 13: 14: 14) rows, ending with a **RS** (WS: WS: WS: **RS**: **RS**) row. 12 sts.
Fasten off.

MAKING UP
Press all pieces with a warm iron over a damp cloth.
Join both shoulder seams using back stitch or mattress stitch if preferred. Join side seams.
Outer edging
With RS facing and using 5.50mm (US I9) hook, attach yarn at upper edge of right back vent opening, 1 ch (does NOT count as st), now work 1 row of dc down right back vent opening edge, across foundation ch edge to front opening edge, up right front opening edge, around neck edge, down left front opening edge, across left foundation edge, and then up left back vent opening edge, working 3 dc into each corner point, do NOT turn.
Now work 1 row of crab st (dc worked from left to right instead of right to left) along this edge.
Fasten off.

Pocket edgings (both alike)

Work edging across all pocket opening edges in same way as given for outer edging.
Neatly sew pocket linings in place on inside.

Sleeve edgings (both alike)

Work edging across foundation ch edge of sleeves in same way as given for outer edging.

Epaulettes (make 2)

Cast on 7 sts using 4mm (US 6) needles.
Work in g st for 28 (28: 28: 30: 30: 30) rows, ending with a WS row.
Cast off.
Lay epaulette over shoulder seam so that cast-on edge matches armhole edge and sew in place along armhole edge.

Sleeve tabs (make 2)

Cast on 8 sts using 4mm (US 6) needles.
Work in g st for 60 (62: 62: 64: 66: 66) rows, ending with a WS row.
Cast off.
Join sleeve seams, enclosing cast-on edge of sleeve tab in seam approx 5 cm up from lower edge of sleeve. Join side seams. Sew sleeves into armholes.
Sew 5 buttons onto left front as in photograph, using "holes" of patt as buttonholes.
Using photograph as a guide, secure free end of epaulette to shoulder seam by attaching a button through epaulette and shoulder seam.
In same way, secure free end of sleeve tabs to sleeves by attaching a button through both layers as in photograph. Attach buttons to close pocket opening edges in same way, using photograph as a guide.

58 (60: 60: 60: 62: 62) cm
23 (23½: 23½: 23½: 24½: 24½) in

41 (44: 47: 50: 53: 56) cm
16¼ (17¼: 18½: 19½: 20¾: 22) in

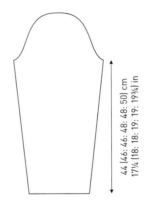

44 (46: 46: 48: 48: 50) cm
17¼ (18: 18: 19: 19: 19¾) in

FLETCHER

Snug coat with cables & generous collar

Recommendation

Suitable for the knitter with a little experience
Please see pages 47, 48 & 49 for photographs.

	XS	S	M	L	XL	XXL	
To fit	**81**	**86**	**91**	**97**	**102**	**109**	cm
bust	32	34	36	38	40	43	in

Rowan Alpaca Chunky

	14	15	15	16	17	18 x 100gm

Photographed in Pigeon

Needles

1 pair 10mm (no 000) (US 15) needles
1 pair 12mm (US 17) needles
Cable needle

Buttons – 6

Tension

10 sts and 14 rows to 10 cm measured over
st st using 10mm (US 15) needles.

Special abbreviations

C4B = slip next 2 sts onto cn and leave at back
of work, K2, then K2 from cn; **C4F** = slip next 2
sts onto cn and leave at front of work, K2, then
K2 from cn; **C6B** = slip next 3 sts onto cn and
leave at back of work, K3, then K3 from cn;
C6F = slip next 3 sts onto cn and leave at front
of work, K3, then K3 from cn; **Cr4LP** = slip
next 3 sts onto cn and leave at front of work,
P1, then K3 from cn; **Cr4RP** = slip next st onto
cn and leave at back of work, K3, then P1 from
cn; **Cr4LK** = slip next 3 sts onto cn and leave
at front of work, K1, then K3 from cn; **Cr4RK** =
slip next st onto cn and leave at back of work,
K3, then K1 from cn; **cn** = cable needle.

BACK

Cast on 70 (72: 74: 78: 80: 84) sts using
10mm (US 15) needles.
Row 1 (RS): K0 (0: 0: 0: 0: 1), P0 (1: 2:
0: 1: 2), (K2, P2) 2 (2: 2: 3: 3: 3) times,
(K4, P2) twice, K3, P3, K2, P3, K3, P2, K3,
P3, K2, P3, K3, (P2, K4) twice, (P2, K2) 2
(2: 2: 3: 3: 3) times, P0 (1: 2: 0: 1: 2), K0
(0: 0: 0: 0: 1).
Row 2: P0 (0: 0: 0: 0: 1), K0 (1: 2: 0: 1: 2),
(P2, K2) 2 (2: 2: 3: 3: 3) times, (P4, K2) twice,
P3, K3, P2, K3, P3, K2, P3, K3, P2, K3, P3,
(K2, P4) twice, (K2, P2) 2 (2: 2: 3: 3: 3) times,
K0 (1: 2: 0: 1: 2), P0 (0: 0: 0: 0: 1).
Rows 3 and 4: As rows 1 and 2.
Row 5: K0 (0: 0: 0: 0: 1), P0 (1: 2: 0: 1: 2),
(K2, P2) 2 (2: 2: 3: 3: 3) times, (C4F, P2) twice,
K3, P3, K2, P3, K3, P2, K3, P3, K2, P3, K3,
(P2, C4B) twice, (P2, K2) 2 (2: 2: 3: 3: 3)
times, P0 (1: 2: 0: 1: 2), K0 (0: 0: 0: 0: 1).
Row 6: As row 2.
Rows 7 and 8: As rows 1 and 2.
Now work in main patt, placing cable panels
as folls:

Row 1 (RS): K8 (9: 10: 12: 13: 15), (K4, P2)
twice, work next 14 sts as row 1 of cable panel
A, P2, work next 14 sts as row 1 of cable panel
B, (P2, K4) twice, K8 (9: 10: 12: 13: 15).
Row 2: K8 (9: 10: 12: 13: 15), (P4, K2) twice,
work next 14 sts as row 2 of cable panel B,
K2, work next 14 sts as row 2 of cable panel A,
(K2, P4) twice, K8 (9: 10: 12: 13: 15).
These 2 rows set position of cable panels with
2 sts in rev st st between panels.
Working appropriate rows of cable panels, cont
as folls:
Row 3: K8 (9: 10: 12: 13: 15), (K4, P2) twice,
patt 30 sts, (P2, K4) twice, K8 (9: 10: 12: 13: 15).
Row 4: K8 (9: 10: 12: 13: 15), (P4, K2) twice,
patt 30 sts, (K2, P4) twice, K8 (9: 10: 12: 13: 15).
Row 5: K8 (9: 10: 12: 13: 15), (C4F, P2) twice,
patt 30 sts, (P2, C4B) twice, K8 (9: 10: 12: 13: 15).
Row 6: As row 4.
Rows 7 and 8: As rows 3 and 4.
Last 8 rows form patt for side sts - 2 cables
each side with edge sts in g st.
Cont as now set until back measures 65 (65:
65: 66: 66: 66) cm, ending with a WS row.

Cable Panel B

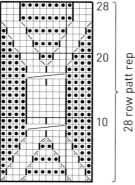

Cable Panel A

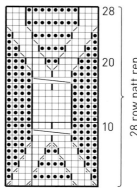

KEY

☐	K on RS, P on WS
▪	P on RS, K on WS
▱	C6B
▱	C6F
▱	Cr4RK
▱	Cr4LK
▱	Cr4RP
▱	Cr4LP

Shape armholes

Keeping patt correct, cast off 4 sts at beg of next 2 rows. 62 (64: 66: 70: 72: 76) sts.

Dec 1 st at each end of next 5 (5: 5: 7: 7: 9) rows, then on foll 1 (2: 2: 2: 2: 2) alt rows, then on foll 4th row. 48 (48: 50: 50: 52: 52) sts.

Cont straight until armhole measures 20 (21: 22: 22: 23: 24) cm, ending with a WS row.

Shape shoulders and back neck

Cast off 4 (4: 5: 4: 5: 5) sts at beg of next 2 rows. 40 (40: 40: 42: 42: 42) sts.

Next row (RS): Cast off 4 (4: 5: 4: 5: 5) sts, patt until there are 8 (8: 7: 8: 7: 7) sts on right needle and turn, leaving rem sts on a holder.

Work each side of neck separately.

Cast off 3 sts at beg of next row.

Cast off rem 5 (5: 4: 5: 4: 4) sts.

With RS facing, rejoin yarn to rem sts, cast off centre 16 (16: 16: 18: 18: 18) sts, patt to end.

Complete to match first side, rev shapings.

LEFT FRONT

Cast on 41 (42: 43: 45: 46: 48) sts using 10mm (US 15) needles.

Row 1 (RS): K0 (0: 0: 0: 0: 1), P0 (1: 2: 0: 1: 2), (K2, P2) 2 (2: 2: 3: 3: 3) times, (K4, P2) twice, K3, P3, K2, P3, K3, P2, K5.

Row 2: K7, P3, K3, P2, K3, P3, (K2, P4) twice, (K2, P2) 2 (2: 2: 3: 3: 3) times, K0 (1: 2: 0: 1: 2), P0 (0: 0: 0: 0: 1).

Rows 3 and 4: As rows 1 and 2.

Row 5: K0 (0: 0: 0: 0: 1), P0 (1: 2: 0: 1: 2), (K2, P2) 2 (2: 2: 3: 3: 3) times, (C4F, P2) twice, K3, P3, K2, P3, K3, P2, K5.

Row 6: As row 2.

Rows 7 and 8: As rows 1 and 2.

Now work in main patt, placing cable panel as folls:

Row 1 (RS): K8 (9: 10: 12: 13: 15), (K4, P2) twice, work next 14 sts as row 1 of cable panel A, P2, K5.

Row 2: K7, work next 14 sts as row 2 of cable panel A, (K2, P4) twice, K8 (9: 10: 12: 13: 15).

These 2 rows set position of cable panel and front opening edge sts in g st, with 2 sts in rev st st between.

Keeping front opening edge sts correct as now set and working appropriate rows of cable panel, cont as folls:

Row 3: K8 (9: 10: 12: 13: 15), (K4, P2) twice, patt 21 sts.

Row 4: Patt 21 sts, (K2, P4) twice, K8 (9: 10: 12: 13: 15).

Row 5: K8 (9: 10: 12: 13: 15), (C4F, P2) twice, patt 21 sts.

Row 6: As row 4.

Rows 7 and 8: As rows 3 and 4.

Last 8 rows form patt for side sts - 2 cables with edge sts in g st.

Cont as now set until left front matches back to start of armhole shaping, ending with a WS row.

Shape armhole

Keeping patt correct, cast off 4 sts at beg of next row. 37 (38: 39: 41: 42: 44) sts.

Work 1 row.

Dec 1 st at armhole edge of next 5 (5: 5: 7: 7: 9) rows, then on foll 1 (2: 2: 2: 2: 2) alt rows, then on foll 4th row.

30 (30: 31: 31: 32: 32) sts.

Cont straight until 8 (8: 8: 10: 10: 10) rows less have been worked than on back to start of shoulder shaping, ending with a WS row.

Shape front neck

Next row (RS): Patt 19 (19: 20: 20: 21: 21) sts and turn, leaving rem 11 sts on a holder.

Keeping patt correct, dec 1 st at neck edge of next 4 rows, then on foll 1 (1: 1: 2: 2: 2) alt rows.

14 (14: 15: 14: 15: 15) sts.

Work 1 row, ending with a WS row.

Shape shoulder

Cast off 4 (4: 5: 4: 5: 5) sts at beg of next and foll alt row **and at same time** dec 1 st at neck edge of next row.

Work 1 row.

Cast off rem 5 (5: 4: 5: 4: 4) sts.

Mark positions for 5 buttons along left front opening edge - first to come in row 31, last to come in neck shaping row, and rem 3 buttons evenly spaced between.

RIGHT FRONT

Cast on 41 (42: 43: 45: 46: 48) sts using 10mm (US 15) needles.

Row 1 (RS): K5, P2, K3, P3, K2, P3, K3, (P2, K4) twice, (P2, K2) 2 (2: 2: 3: 3: 3) times, P0 (1: 2: 0: 1: 2), K0 (0: 0: 0: 0: 1).

Row 2: P0 (0: 0: 0: 0: 1), K0 (1: 2: 0: 1: 2), (P2, K2) 2 (2: 2: 3: 3: 3) times, (P4, K2) twice, P3, K3, P2, K3, P3, K7.

Rows 3 and 4: As rows 1 and 2.

Row 5: K5, P2, K3, P3, K2, P3, K3, (P2, C4B) twice, (P2, K2) 2 (2: 2: 3: 3: 3) times, P0 (1: 2: 0: 1: 2), K0 (0: 0: 0: 0: 1).

Row 6: As row 2.

Rows 7 and 8: As rows 1 and 2.

Now work in main patt, placing cable panels as folls:

Row 1 (RS): K5, P2, work next 14 sts as row 1 of cable panel B, (P2, K4) twice, K8 (9: 10: 12: 13: 15).

Row 2: K8 (9: 10: 12: 13: 15), (P4, K2) twice, work next 14 sts as row 2 of cable panel B, K7.

These 2 rows set position of cable panel and front opening edge sts in g st, with 2 sts in rev st st between.

Keeping front opening edge sts correct as now set and working appropriate rows of cable panel, cont as folls:

Row 3: Patt 21 sts, (P2, K4) twice, K8 (9: 10: 12: 13: 15).

Row 4: K8 (9: 10: 12: 13: 15), (P4, K2) twice, patt 21 sts.

Row 5: Patt 21 sts, (P2, C4B) twice, K8 (9: 10: 12: 13: 15).

Row 6: As row 4.

Rows 7 and 8: As rows 3 and 4.

Last 8 rows form patt for side sts - 2 cables with edge sts in g st.

Cont as now set for a further 14 rows, ending with a WS row.

Next row (buttonhole row) (RS): K1, K2tog, yfwd (to make a buttonhole), patt to end.

Working a further 3 buttonholes in this way and noting that no further reference will be made to buttonholes, complete to match left front, reversing shapings and working first row of neck shaping as folls:

Shape front neck

Next row (RS): K1, K2tog, yfwd (to make 5th buttonhole), patt 8 sts and slip these 11 sts onto another holder, patt to end.

19 (19: 20: 20: 21: 21) sts.

LEFT SLEEVE

Cast on 30 (30: 32: 32: 34: 34) sts using 10mm (US 15) needles.

Row 1 (RS): K0 (0: 1: 1: 2: 2), P2, K4, P2, K3, P3, K2, P3, K3, P2, K4, P2, K0 (0: 1: 1: 2: 2).

Row 2: P0 (0: 1: 1: 2: 2), K2, P4, K2, P3, K3, P2, K3, P3, K2, P4, K2, P0 (0: 1: 1: 2: 2).

Rows 3 and 4: As rows 1 and 2.

Row 5: K0 (0: 1: 1: 2: 2), P2, C4F, P2, K3, P3, K2, P3, K3, P2, C4B, P2, K0 (0: 1: 1: 2: 2).

Row 6: As row 2.

Now place cable panel as folls:

Row 7: K0 (0: 1: 1: 2: 2), P2, K4, P2, work next 14 sts as row 27 of cable panel B, P2, K4, P2, K0 (0: 1: 1: 2: 2).

Row 8: P0 (0: 1: 1: 2: 2), K2, P4, K2, work next 14 sts as row **28** of cable panel B, K2, P4, K2, P0 (0: 1: 1: 2: 2).

These 2 rows set position of cable panel with 2 sts in rev st st either side.

Working appropriate rows of cable panel, cont as folls:

Row 9: K0 (0: 1: 1: 2: 2), P2, K4, patt 18 sts, K4, P2, K0 (0: 1: 1: 2: 2).

Row 10: P0 (0: 1: 1: 2: 2), K2, P4, patt 18 sts, P4, K2, P0 (0: 1: 1: 2: 2).

Now work in main patt as folls:

Row 1 (RS): Inc in first st, K5 (5: 6: 6: 7: 7), patt 18 sts, K5 (5: 6: 6: 7: 7), inc in last st. 32 (32: 34: 34: 36: 36) sts.

Row 2 and every foll alt row: K3 (3: 4: 4: 5: 5), P4, patt 18 sts, P4, K3 (3: 4: 4: 5: 5).

Row 3: K3 (3: 4: 4: 5: 5), C4F, patt 18 sts, C4B, K3 (3: 4: 4: 5: 5).

Row 5: K7 (7: 8: 8: 9: 9), patt 18 sts, K7 (7: 8: 8: 9: 9).

Row 7: As row 5.

Row 8: As row 2.

Last 8 rows form patt for side sts - 2 cables with edge sts in g st - and beg sleeve shaping. Cont as now set, shaping sides by inc 1 st at each end of next and foll 8th row, then on 3 foll 10th rows, taking inc sts into g st. 42 (42: 44: 44: 46: 46) sts.

Cont straight until sleeve measures 46 (47: 48: 49: 50: 51) cm, ending with a WS row.

Shape top

Keeping patt correct, cast off 4 sts at beg of next 2 rows.

34 (34: 36: 36: 38: 38) sts.

Dec 1 st at each end of next and 2 foll 4th rows. 28 (28: 30: 30: 32: 32) sts.

Work 3 rows, ending with a WS row.

Dec 1 st at each end of next and every foll alt row to 22 sts, then on foll 3 rows, ending with a WS row.

Cast off rem 16 sts.

RIGHT SLEEVE

Work as given for left sleeve, placing cable panel A instead of cable panel B.

MAKING UP

Press all pieces with a warm iron over a damp cloth.

Join both shoulder seams using back stitch or mattress stitch if preferred.

Collar

With RS facing and using 10mm (US 15) needles, slip 11 sts on right front holder onto right needle, rejoin yarn and pick up and knit 11 (11: 11: 14: 14: 14) sts up right side of neck, 20 (20: 20: 22: 22: 22) sts from back, and 11 (11: 11: 14: 14: 14) sts down left side of neck, then patt 11 sts on left front holder. 64 (64: 64: 72: 72: 72) sts.

Row 1 (RS of collar, WS of body): K7, *P2, K2, rep from * to last 5 sts, K5.

Row 2: K5, *P2, K2, rep from * to last 3 sts, K3. These 2 rows set the sts - 5 sts at each end of rows still in g st with all other sts in rib. Cont as set for a further 5 rows, ending with **WS** of collar (RS of body) facing for next row.

Row 8 (WS of collar): K1, K2tog tbl, yfwd (to make 6th buttonhole), patt to end. Work 2 rows.

Row 11 (RS of collar): K6, M1, K1, *P2, K1, M1, K1, rep from * to last 5 sts, K5. 78 (78: 78: 88: 88: 88) sts.

Row 12: K5, *P3, K2, rep from * to last 3 sts, K3.

Row 13: K8, *P2, K3, rep from * to last 5 sts, K5. Rep last 2 rows 6 times more. Change to 12mm (US 17) needles. Work a further 6 rows. Cast off in patt (on **WS** of collar). Join side seams. Join sleeve seams. Sew sleeves into armholes. Sew on buttons.

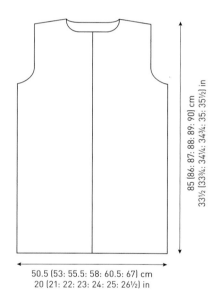

50.5 (53: 55.5: 58: 60.5: 67) cm
20 (21: 22: 23: 24: 25: 26½) in

85 [86: 87: 88: 89: 90] cm
33½ (33¾: 34¼: 34¾: 35: 35½) in

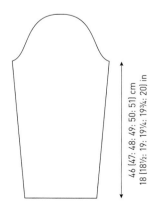

46 (47: 48: 49: 50: 51) cm
18 (18½: 19: 19¼: 19¾: 20) in

Recommendation

Suitable for the knitter with a little experience
Please see page 26 & 27 for photographs.

	XS	S	M	L	XL	XXL	
To fit	**81**	**86**	**91**	**97**	**102**	**109**	**cm**
bust	32	34	36	38	40	43	in

Rowan Felted Tweed Chunky

	23	24	26	28	29	31	x 50gm

Photographed in Ink

Needles

1 pair 6mm (no 4) (US 10) needles
1 pair 7mm (no 2) (US 10½/11) needles
5.00mm (no 6) (US H8) crochet hook

Buttons – 9

Tension

12 sts and 18 rows to 10 cm measured over
textured pattern using 7mm (US 10½/11)
needles.

Crochet abbreviations

ch = chain; **dc** = double crochet; **ss** = slip
stitch.

HARRIS
Textured coat with epaulets & crochet trims

BACK

Cast on 69 (73: 77: 79: 83: 87) sts using
7mm (US 10½/11) needles.
Row 1 (RS): K1, *P1, K1, rep from * to end.
Row 2: As row 1.
Row 3: P1, *K1, P1, rep from * to end.
Row 4: As row 3.
These 4 rows form double moss st.
Work in double moss st for a further 2 (2: 2:
4: 4: 4) rows, ending with a WS row.
Now work in textured patt as folls:
Work in double moss st as set for 12 rows,
ending with a WS row.
Row 13 (RS): Purl.
Row 14: Knit.
Last 14 rows form textured patt.
Keeping patt correct, dec 1 st at each end of
9th and 2 foll 8th rows, then on 3 foll 6th
rows, then on 4 foll 4th rows.
49 (53: 57: 59: 63: 67) sts.
Work 17 rows, ending with a WS row.
Inc 1 st at each end of next and foll 10th
row, then on foll 8th row.
55 (59: 63: 65: 69: 73) sts.
Work 9 rows, ending after patt row 6 and
with a WS row.
(Back should measure 69 (69: 69: 70: 70:
70) cm.)
Shape armholes
Keeping patt correct, cast off 3 sts at beg
of next 2 rows.
49 (53: 57: 59: 63: 67) sts.
Dec 1 st at each end of next 1 (1: 3: 3: 5: 5)
rows, then on foll 1 (2: 1: 2: 1: 2) alt rows, then
on foll 4th row. 43 (45: 47: 47: 49: 51) sts.
Cont straight until armhole measures 19 (20:
21: 21: 22: 23) cm, ending with a WS row.
Shape shoulders and back neck
Cast off 4 (4: 4: 4: 4: 5) sts at beg of next
2 rows. 35 (37: 39: 39: 41: 41) sts.
Next row (RS): Cast off 4 (4: 4: 4: 4: 5) sts,
patt until there are 7 (8: 9: 8: 9: 8) sts on right
needle and turn, leaving rem sts on a holder.
Work each side of neck separately.
Cast off 4 sts at beg of next row.
Cast off rem 3 (4: 5: 4: 5: 4) sts.
With RS facing, rejoin yarn to rem sts, cast off
centre 13 (13: 13: 15: 15: 15) sts, patt to end.
Complete to match first side, reversing
shapings.

LEFT FRONT

Cast on 40 (42: 44: 45: 47: 49) sts using
7mm (US 10½/11) needles.
Row 1 (RS): *K1, P1, rep from * to last 0 (0: 0:
1: 1: 1) st, K0 (0: 0: 1: 1: 1).
Row 2: K0 (0: 0: 1: 1: 1), *P1, K1, rep from *
to end.
Row 3: *P1, K1, rep from * to last 0 (0: 0:
1: 1: 1) st, P0 (0: 0: 1: 1: 1).
Row 4: P0 (0: 0: 1: 1: 1), *K1, P1, rep from *
to end.
These 4 rows form double moss st.
Work in double moss st for a further 2 (2: 2:
4: 4: 4) rows, ending with a WS row.
Now work in textured patt as folls:
Work in double moss st as set for 12 rows,
ending with a WS row.
Row 13 (RS): Purl.
Row 14: Knit.
Last 14 rows form textured patt.
Keeping patt correct, dec 1 st at beg of 9th
and 2 foll 8th rows, then on 3 foll 6th rows,
then on 4 foll 4th rows.
30 (32: 34: 35: 37: 39) sts.
Work 17 rows, ending with a WS row.
Inc 1 st at beg of next and foll 10th row,
then on foll 8th row.
33 (35: 37: 38: 40: 42) sts.
Work 9 rows, ending after patt row 6 and
with a WS row.
Shape armhole
Keeping patt correct, cast off 3 sts at beg
of next 2 rows.
30 (32: 34: 35: 37: 39) sts.
Work 1 row.
Dec 1 st at armhole edge of next 1 (1: 3:
3: 5: 5) rows, then on foll 1 (2: 1: 2: 1: 2)
alt rows, then on foll 4th row.
27 (28: 29: 29: 30: 31) sts.
Cont straight until 9 (9: 9: 11: 11: 11) rows
less have been worked than on back to beg
of shoulder shaping, ending with a **RS** row.
Shape front neck
Keeping patt correct, cast off 11 sts at beg
of next row.
16 (17: 18: 18: 19: 20) sts.
Dec 1 st at neck edge of next 3 rows, then
on 2 (2: 2: 3: 3: 3) alt rows.
11 (12: 13: 12: 13: 14) sts.
Work 1 row, ending with a WS row.

Shape shoulder

Cast off 4 (4: 4: 4: 4: 5) sts at beg of next and foll alt row.

Work 1 row.

Cast off rem 3 (4: 5: 4: 5: 4) sts.

Mark positions for 5 buttons along left front opening edge - first to come in row 37 (37: 37: 39: 39: 39), last to come 2 cm below neck shaping, and rem 3 buttons evenly spaced between.

RIGHT FRONT

Cast on 40 (42: 44: 45: 47: 49) sts using 7mm (US 10½/11) needles.

Row 1 (RS): K0 (0: 0: 1: 1: 1), *P1, K1, rep from * to end.

Row 2: *K1, P1, rep from * to last 0 (0: 0: 1: 1: 1) st, K0 (0: 0: 1: 1: 1).

Row 3: P0 (0: 0: 1: 1: 1), *K1, P1, rep from * to end.

Row 4: *P1, K1, rep from * to last 0 (0: 0: 1: 1: 1) st, P0 (0: 0: 1: 1: 1).

These 4 rows form double moss st.

Work in double moss st for a further 2 (2: 2: 4: 4: 4) rows, ending with a WS row.

Now work in textured patt as folls:

Work in double moss st as set for 12 rows, ending with a WS row.

Row 13 (RS): Purl.

Row 14: Knit.

Last 14 rows form textured patt.

Keeping patt correct, dec 1 st at beg of 9th row.

39 (41: 43: 44: 46: 48) sts.

Work 7 rows, ending with a WS row.

Next row (buttonhole row) (RS): Patt 2 sts, work 2 tog tbl, yrn (to make a buttonhole), patt to last 2 sts, work 2 tog.

Making a further 4 buttonholes in this way to correspond with positions marked for buttons, complete to match left front, reversing shapings.

SLEEVES (both alike)

Cast on 31 (33: 35: 35: 37: 39) sts using 7mm (US 10½/11) needles.

Work in double moss st as given for back for 4 (4: 6: 8: 10: 12) rows, ending with a WS row.

Next row (RS): Purl.

Next row: Knit.

Last 6 (6: 8: 10: 12: 14) rows set position of patt as given for back.

Cont in patt, shaping sides by inc 1 st at each end of 13th (13th: 11th: 9th: 7th: 5th) and 3 foll 18th rows, taking inc sts into patt.

39 (41: 43: 43: 45: 47) sts.

Work 9 (9: 11: 13: 15: 17) rows, ending after patt row 6 and with a WS row. (Sleeve should measure 46 (46: 47: 48: 49: 50) cm.)

Shape top

Keeping patt correct, cast off 3 sts at beg of next 2 rows.

33 (35: 37: 37: 39: 41) sts.

Dec 1 st at each end of next and foll alt row, then on 3 foll 4th rows, then on foll 1 (2: 3: 3: 4: 5) alt rows, then on foll 5 rows, ending with a WS row.

Cast off rem 11 sts.

MAKING UP

Press all pieces with a warm iron over a damp cloth.

Join both shoulder seams using back stitch or mattress stitch if preferred.

Epaulettes (make 2)

Cast on 7 sts using 6mm (US 10) needles.

Work in g st for 24 (26: 28: 26: 28: 30) rows, ending with a WS row.

Cast off.

Lay epaulette over shoulder seam so that cast-on edge matches armhole edge and sew in place along armhole edge.

Sleeve tabs (make 2)

Cast on 7 sts using 6mm (US 10) needles.

Work in g st for 44 (46: 48: 48: 50: 52) rows, ending with a WS row.

Cast off.

Join sleeve seams, enclosing cast-on edge of sleeve tab in seam approx 4 cm up from sleeve cast-on edge. Join side seams.

Sew sleeves into armholes.

Body edging

With RS facing and using 5.00mm (US H8) hook, attach yarn at base of left side seam, 1 ch (does NOT count as st), now work 1 round of dc around entire hem, front opening and neck edges, working 3 dc into each corner point and ending with ss to first dc, do NOT turn.

Now work 1 round of crab st (dc worked from left to right instead of right to left) around edge.

Fasten off.

Cuff edgings

Work around cast-on edges of sleeves as given for body edging, attaching yarn at base of sleeve seam.

Sew 5 buttons onto left front to correspond with buttonholes.

Using photograph as a guide, secure free end of epaulette to shoulder seam by attaching a button through epaulette and shoulder seam.

In same way, secure free end of sleeve tabs to sleeves by attaching a button through both layers as in photograph.

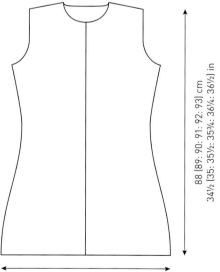

46 [48.5: 51: 53.5: 56: 60] cm
18 [19: 20: 21: 22: 23½] in

88 [89: 90: 91: 92: 93] cm
34½ [35: 35½: 35¾: 36¼: 36½] in

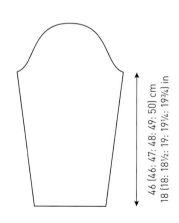

46 [46: 47: 48: 49: 50] cm
18 [18: 18½: 19: 19¼: 19¾] in

BLAKE
Ribbed Sloppy Joe with cosy neckline

Recommendation
Suitable for the knitter with a little experience
Please see pages 29, 30 & 31 for photographs.

	XS	S	M	L	XL	XXL	
To fit	**81**	**86**	**91**	**97**	**102**	**109**	**cm**
bust	32	34	36	38	40	43	**in**

Rowan Alpaca Chunky

11	11	12	12	13	13 x 100gm

Photographed in Wren

Needles
1 pair 9mm (no 00) (US 13) needles
1 pair 10mm (no 000) (US 15) needles

Tension
10 sts and 15 rows to 10 cm measured over
pattern using 10mm (US 15) needles.

BACK and FRONT (both alike)
Cast on 59 (61: 63: 67: 69: 73) sts using
10mm (US 15) needles.
Row 1 (RS): K3 (0: 3: 3: 0: 0), *P1, K3,
rep from * to last 0 (1: 0: 0: 1: 1) st,
P0 (1: 0: 0: 1: 1).
Row 2: K1 (2: 1: 1: 2: 2), *P1, K3, rep
from * to last 2 (3: 2: 2: 3: 3) sts, P1,
K1 (2: 1: 1: 2: 2).
These 2 rows form patt.
Cont in patt until work measures 35 (36: 36:
37: 36: 37) cm, ending with a WS row.
Shape raglan armholes
Keeping patt correct, cast off 3 (4: 3: 3: 4: 4)
sts at beg of next 2 rows.
53 (53: 57: 61: 61: 65) sts.
Work 2 (2: 2: 0: 2: 0) rows.
Sizes XS, S and M only
Next row (RS): P1, K3, P2tog, patt to last
6 sts, P2tog tbl, K3, P1.
Next row: K2, P1, K2, patt to last 5 sts, K2, P1, K2.
Next row: P1, K3, P1, patt to last 5 sts, P1,
K3, P1.
Next row: K2, P1, K2, patt to last 5 sts, K2, P1, K2.
Rep last 4 rows 1 (1: 0: -: -: -) times more.
49 (49: 55: -: -: -) sts.
Size XXL only
Next row (RS): P1, K3, P2tog, patt to last
6 sts, P2tog tbl, K3, P1.
Next row: K2, P1, K1, K2tog tbl, patt to last
6 sts, K2tog, K1, P1, K2. 61 sts.
All sizes
Next row (RS): P1, K3, P2tog, patt to last
6 sts, P2tog tbl, K3, P1.
Next row: K2, P1, K2, patt to last 5 sts, K2, P1, K2.
Rep last 2 rows 11 (11: 14: 17: 17: 17) times
more, ending with a WS row.
Cast off rem 25 sts.

SLEEVES (both alike)
Cast on 51 (53: 55: 55: 57: 57) sts using
10mm (US 15) needles.
Cont in patt as given for back and front until
sleeve measures 33 (34: 35: 36: 37: 38) cm,
ending with a WS row.
Shape raglans
Keeping patt correct, cast off 3 (4: 3: 3:
4: 4) sts at beg of next 2 rows.
45 (45: 49: 49: 49: 49) sts.
Work 2 (2: 0: 0: 2: 2) rows.

Next row (RS): P1, K3, P2tog, patt to last
6 sts, P2tog tbl, K3, P1.
Next row: K2, P1, K2, patt to last 5 sts, K2,
P1, K2.
Rep last 2 rows 14 (14: 16: 16: 16: 16) times
more, ending with a WS row. 15 sts.
Next row (RS): P1, K3, P2tog, patt 3 sts,
P2tog tbl, K3, P1.
Next row: K2, P1, K1, K2tog tbl, patt 1 st,
K2tog, K1, P1, K2.
Cast off rem 11 sts.

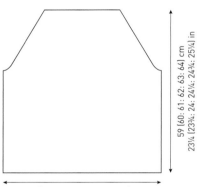

59 (60: 61: 62: 63: 64) cm
23¼ (23¾: 24: 24¼: 24¾: 25¼) in

53.5 (56: 58.5: 61: 63.5: 67.5) cm
21 (22: 23: 24: 25: 26½) in

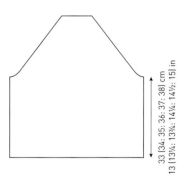

33 (34: 35: 36: 37: 38) cm
13 (13½: 13¾: 14¼: 14½: 15) in

Continued on next page...

Recommendation
Suitable for the novice knitter
Please see page 34 for photograph.

Rowan Cocoon
4   x 100gm
Photographed in Alpine

Needles
1 pair 6½mm (no 3) (US 10½) needles
Cable needle

Tension
20 sts and 22 rows to 10 cm measured over
pattern using 6½mm (US 10½) needles.

Finished size
Completed scarf measures 21.5 cm (8½ ins)
wide and is approx 164 cm (64½ ins) long.

THUNDER
Classic cable & rib scarf

SCARF
Cast on 39 sts using 6½mm (US 10½)
needles.
Row 1 (RS): K2, (P1, K3) 3 times, P1, (K1, inc
in next st) twice, P1, (K1, inc in next st) twice,
P1, (K3, P1) 3 times, K2. 43 sts.
Now work in patt as folls:
Row 1: K4, (P1, K3) twice, P1, K2, P6, K1, P6,
K2, P1, (K3, P1) twice, K4.
Row 2: K2, (P1, K3) 3 times, (P1, K6) twice,
P1, (K3, P1) 3 times, K2.
Rows 3 to 10: As rows 1 and 2, 4 times.
Row 11: As row 1.
Row 12: K2, (P1, K3) 3 times, P1, slip next
3 sts onto cable needle and leave at back of
work, K3, then K3 from cable needle, P1, slip
next 3 sts onto cable needle and leave at front
of work, K3, then K3 from cable needle, P1,
(K3, P1) 3 times, K2.
Rows 13 to 16: As rows 1 and 2, twice.
These 16 rows form patt.
Cont in patt until scarf measures approx 164
cm, ending after patt row 6 and with a **RS** row.
Next row (WS): K4, (P1, K3) twice, P1, K2, (P1,
P2tog) twice, K1, (P1, P2tog) twice, K2, P1, (K3,
P1) twice, K4. 39 sts.
Cast off in patt.

BLAKE– Continued from previous page.

MAKING UP
Press all pieces with a warm iron over
a damp cloth.
Join all raglan seams using back stitch
or mattress stitch if preferred.
Collar
Cast on 89 sts using 10mm (US 15) needles.
Row 1 (RS): K1, *P1, K3, rep from * to end.
Row 2: As row 1.
These 2 rows form patt.
Work in patt for a further 8 rows, ending with
a WS row.

Counting in from **end** of last row, place markers
on 8th and 52nd sts - 2 markers in total and 37
sts beyond 2nd marker at opposite end of row.
Row 11 (RS): *Patt to within 3 sts of marked
st, P2tog, patt 3 sts (marked st is centre st of
these 3 sts), P2tog tbl, rep from * once more,
patt to end. 85 sts.
Row 12: *Patt to within 2 sts of marked st,
K2, P marked st, K2, rep from * once more,
patt to end.
Row 13: *Patt to within 2 sts of marked st,
P1, K3 (marked st is centre st of these 3 sts),

P1, rep from * once more, patt to end.
Rows 14 and 15: As rows 12 and 13.
Row 16: As row 12.
Rep rows 11 to 16, twice more, then row
11 again, ending with a RS row. 73 sts.
Change to 9mm (US 13) needles.
Work 7 rows, ending with a WS row.
Cast off.
Join row-end edges of collar.
Matching marked sts to centre of top
of sleeves, sew cast-off edge of collar
to neck edge. Join side and sleeve seams.

SETH

Classic sweater with buttoned shoulder detail

Recommendation

Suitable for the knitter with a little experience
Please see pages 36 & 37 for photographs.

	XS	S	M	L	XL	XXL	
To fit	**81**	**86**	**91**	**97**	**102**	**109**	cm
bust	32	34	36	38	40	43	in

Rowan Kid Classic

	9	10	11	12	13	14	x 50gm

Photographed in Nightly

Needles

1 pair 4mm (no 8) (US 6) needles
1 pair 4½mm (no 7) (US 7) needles

Buttons – 5

Tension

21 sts and 27 rows to 10 cm measured over
stocking stitch using 4½mm (US 7) needles.

BACK

Cast on 98 (102: 110: 114: 118: 126) sts
using 4mm (US 6) needles.
Row 1 (RS): P2, *K2, P2, rep from * to end.
Row 2: K2, *P2, K2, rep from * to end.
These 2 rows form rib.
Cont in rib until back measures 9 cm, dec
1 (0: 1: 1: 0: 0) st at each end of last row
and ending with a WS row.
96 (102: 108: 112: 118: 126) sts.
Change to 4½mm (US 7) needles.
Beg with a K row, work in st st until back
measures 44 (44: 44: 45: 45: 45) cm,
ending with a WS row.
Shape armholes
Cast off 6 sts at beg of next 2 rows.
84 (90: 96: 100: 106: 114) sts.
Cont straight until armhole measures 22 (23:
24: 24: 25: 26) cm, ending with a WS row.
Shape shoulders and back neck
Cast off 7 (8: 9: 9: 10: 12) sts at beg of
next 2 rows.
70 (74: 78: 82: 86: 90) sts.
Next row (RS): Cast off 7 (8: 9: 9: 10: 12) sts,
K until there are 12 (12: 13: 14: 15: 15) sts
on right needle and turn, leaving rem sts on
a holder.
Work each side of neck separately.
Cast off 4 sts at beg of next row.
Cast off rem 8 (8: 9: 10: 11: 11) sts.
With RS facing, rejoin yarn to rem sts, cast off
centre 32 (34: 34: 36: 36: 36) sts, K to end.
Complete to match first side, reversing
shapings.

FRONT

Work as given for back until 16 (16: 16: 18:
18: 18) rows less have been worked than
on back to start of shoulder shaping,
ending with a WS row.
Shape front neck
Next row (RS): K31 (33: 36: 38: 41: 45)
and turn, leaving rem sts on a holder.
Work each side of neck separately.
Dec 1 st at neck edge of next 3 rows,
ending with a WS row.
28 (30: 33: 35: 38: 42) sts.
Cast off.
With RS facing, rejoin yarn to rem sts, cast off
centre 22 (24: 24: 24: 24: 24) sts, K to end.

Dec 1 st at neck edge of next 6 rows, then
on foll 2 (2: 2: 3: 3: 3) alt rows, then on foll
4th row. 22 (24: 27: 28: 31: 35) sts.
Work 2 rows, ending with a **RS** row.
Shape shoulder
Cast off 7 (8: 9: 9: 10: 12) sts at beg of next
and foll alt row.
Work 1 row.
Cast off rem 8 (8: 9: 10: 11: 11) sts.

LEFT SHOULDER SECTION

Cast on 28 (30: 33: 35: 38: 42) sts using
4½mm (US 7) needles.
Beg with a K row, work in st st as folls:
Dec 1 st at end (neck edge) of next row and
at same edge on foll 2 rows, then on foll
2 (2: 2: 3: 3: 3) alt rows, then on foll 4th row.
22 (24: 27: 28: 31: 35) sts.
Work 1 row, ending with a WS row.
Shape shoulder
Cast off 7 (8: 9: 9: 10: 12) sts at beg of next
and foll alt row.
Work 1 row.
Cast off rem 8 (8: 9: 10: 11: 11) sts.

SLEEVES (both alike)

Cast on 60 (62: 64: 66: 68: 70) sts using
4mm (US 6) needles.
Row 1 (RS): P1 (0: 1: 0: 1: 0), *K2, P2, rep from
* to last 3 (2: 3: 2: 3: 2) sts, K2, P1 (0: 1: 0: 1: 0).
Row 2: K1 (0: 1: 0: 1: 0), *P2, K2, rep from * to
last 3 (2: 3: 2: 3: 2) sts, P2, K1 (0: 1: 0: 1: 0).
These 2 rows form rib.
Cont in rib, shaping sides by inc 1 st at each
end of 23rd and 2 (2: 2: 2: 2: 1) foll 8th (8th:
6th: 8th: 8th: 8th) rows, then on 0 (0: 0: 0: 0:
1) foll 6th row. 66 (68: 70: 72: 74: 76) sts.
Work 1 (1: 5: 1: 1: 3) rows, ending with a WS row.
Change to 4½mm (US 7) needles.
Beg with a K row, now work in st st throughout
as folls:
Work 6 (4: 0: 6: 6: 2) rows, ending with a WS row.
Next row (RS): K3, M1, K to last 3 sts, M1, K3.
Working all increases as set by last row, inc
1 st at each end of 8th (6th: 6th: 8th: 6th:
6th) and 0 (0: 0: 1: 0: 0) foll 8th row, then
on every foll 6th row until there are 94 (98:
102: 102: 106: 110) sts.
Work 9 rows, ending with a WS row. (Sleeve
should measure 49 (50: 51: 52: 53: 54) cm.)

Shape top

Place markers at both ends of last row.
Work 8 rows, ending with a WS row.
Cast off 8 sts at beg of next 8 rows.
Cast off rem 30 (34: 38: 38: 42: 46) sts.

MAKING UP

Press all pieces with a warm iron over
a damp cloth.
Join right shoulder seam using back stitch
or mattress stitch if preferred. Sew left
shoulder section to back along shoulder
seam edge.

Left front shoulder buttonhole band

Cast on 9 sts using 4mm (US 6) needles.
Row 1 (RS): K1, (P1, K1) 4 times.
Row 2: As row 1.
These 2 rows form moss st.
Work in moss st for a further 8 (12: 14:
14: 14: 16) rows, ending with a WS row.
Next row (RS): K1, P1, K1, P2tog, yrn
(to make a buttonhole), (P1, K1) twice.
Work 11 (11: 13: 13: 15: 17) rows.
Rep last 12 (12: 14: 14: 16: 18) rows
twice more, ending with a WS row.
Do NOT break yarn.

Neckband

With RS facing and using 4mm (US 6)
needles, work across 9 sts of buttonhole band
as folls: K1, P1, K1, P2tog, yrn (to make 4th
buttonhole), P1, K1, P2tog, pick up and knit
4 sts down left side of neck, 22 (24: 24: 24:
24: 24) sts from front, 20 (20: 20: 21: 23: 23)
sts up right side of neck, 40 (42: 42: 44: 44:
44) sts from back, then 16 (16: 16: 17: 19: 19)
sts down left neck to left shoulder section cast-
on edge. 110 (114: 114: 118: 122: 122) sts.
Row 1 (WS): K2, *P2, K2, rep from * to last
8 sts, moss st 8 sts.
Row 2: Moss st 8 sts, P2, *K2, P2, rep from *
to end.
Last 2 rows set the sts.
Cont as set for a further 9 rows, ending with
a WS row.
Row 12 (RS): K1, P1, K1, P2tog, yrn (to make
5th buttonhole), patt to end.
Work 4 rows, ending with a **RS** row.
Cast off in patt (on **WS**).
Neatly sew row-end edge of buttonhole band
to cast-off edge of left front shoulder. Lay
buttonhole band over left shoulder section
so that cast-on edge of left shoulder section
matches band seam and sew edges together
along armhole edge. Matching sleeve markers
to top of side seams, sew sleeves into
armholes. Join side and sleeve seams.
Sew on buttons.

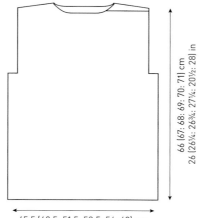

66 (67: 68: 69: 70: 71) cm
26 (26¼: 26¾: 27¼: 27½: 28) in

45.5 (48.5: 51.5: 53.5: 56: 60) cm
18 (19: 20¼: 21: 22: 23½) in

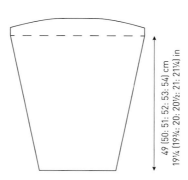

49 (50: 51: 52: 53: 54) cm
19¼ (19¾: 20: 20½: 21: 21¼) in

Recommendation

Suitable for the novice knitter
Please see pages 38 & 39 for photographs

	XS	S	M	L	XL	XXL	
To fit	81	86	91	97	102	109	cm
bust	32	34	36	38	40	43	in

Rowan Kid Classic

| 9 | 10 | 11 | 11 | 12 | 13 | x 50gm |

Photographed in Smoke

Needles

1 pair 3¾mm (no 9) (US 5) needles
1 pair 4mm (no 8) (US 6) needles
1 pair 4½mm (no 7) (US 7) needles

Tension

21 sts and 27 rows to 10 cm measured over
stocking stitch using 4½mm (US 7) needles.

HANLEY

Long-line classic sweater with square set in sleeves

BACK

Cast on 110 (114: 122: 126: 130: 138) sts
using 4mm (US 6) needles.
Row 1 (RS): P2, *K2, P2, rep from * to end.
Row 2: K2, *P2, K2, rep from * to end.
These 2 rows form rib.
Work in rib for a further 38 rows, dec 1 (0: 1: 1:
0: 0) st at each end of last row and ending with
a WS row. 108 (114: 120: 124: 130: 138) sts.
Change to 4½mm (US 7) needles.
Beg with a K row, work in st st until back
measures 48 (48: 48: 49: 49: 49) cm, ending
with a WS row.

Shape armholes

Cast off 5 sts at beg of next 2 rows.
98 (104: 110: 114: 120: 128) sts.
Work 6 (8: 8: 10: 10: 12) rows, ending with
a WS row.
Next row (RS): K3, M1, K to last 3 sts, M1, K3.
Working all increases as set by last row, inc 1 st
at each end of 14th and 2 foll 14th rows.
106 (112: 118: 122: 128: 136) sts.
Cont straight until armhole measures 25 (26:
27: 27: 28: 29) cm, ending with a WS row.

Shape shoulders and back neck

Cast off 7 (8: 9: 9: 10: 12) sts at beg of next
2 rows. 92 (96: 100: 104: 108: 112) sts.
Next row (RS): Cast off 7 (8: 9: 9: 10: 12) sts,
K until there are 12 (12: 13: 14: 15: 15) sts on
right needle and turn, leaving rem sts on a holder.
Work each side of neck separately.
Cast off 4 sts at beg of next row.
Cast off rem 8 (8: 9: 10: 11: 11) sts.
With RS facing, rejoin yarn to rem sts, cast off
centre 54 (56: 56: 58: 58: 58) sts, K to end.
Complete to match first side, reversing shapings.

FRONT

Work as given for back until 8 (8: 8:
10: 10: 10) rows less have been worked than
on back to start of shoulder shaping, ending
with a WS row.

Shape front neck

Next row (RS): K28 (30: 33: 35: 38: 42)
and turn, leaving rem sts on a holder.
Work each side of neck separately.
Dec 1 st at neck edge of next 4 rows, then on
foll 1 (1: 1: 2: 2: 2) alt rows.
23 (25: 28: 29: 32: 36) sts.
Work 1 row, ending with a WS row.

Shape shoulder

Cast off 7 (8: 9: 9: 10: 12) sts at beg of next
and foll alt row **and at same time** dec 1 st at
neck edge of next row.
Work 1 row.
Cast off rem 8 (8: 9: 10: 11: 11) sts.
With RS facing, rejoin yarn to rem sts, cast off
centre 50 (52: 52: 52: 52: 52) sts, K to end.
Complete to match first side, reversing shapings.

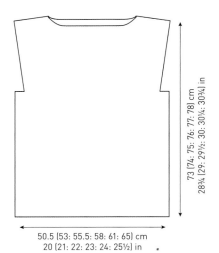

50.5 (53: 55.5: 58: 61: 65) cm
20 (21: 22: 23: 24: 25½) in

73 (74: 75: 76: 77: 78) cm
28¾ (29: 29½: 30: 30¼: 30¾) in

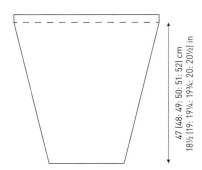

47 (48: 49: 50: 51: 52) cm
18½ (19: 19¾: 20: 20½) in

Continued on next page...

Recommendation

Suitable for the novice knitter
Please see pages 20 & 21 for photographs.

One size

Rowan Baby Alpaca DK

3   x 50gm
Photographed in Southdown

Needles

1 pair 3¼mm (no 10) (US 3) needles
1 pair 4mm (no 8) (US 6) needles

Tension

22 sts and 32 rows to 10 cm measured over
pattern using 4mm (US 6) needles.

TOD
Slouchy ribbed hat

HAT

Cast on 123 sts using 3¼mm (US 3) needles.
Row 1 (RS): K3, *P1, K3, rep from * to end.
Row 2: K1, *P1, K3, rep from * to last 2 sts,
P1, K1.
These 2 rows form patt.
Cont in patt until hat measures 5 cm, ending
with a WS row.
Change to 4mm (US 6) needles.
Cont in patt until hat measures 28 cm, ending
with a WS row.
Shape top
Row 1 (RS): K1, *K1, P3tog, rep from * to last
2 sts, K2. 63 sts.
Row 2: K1, *P1, K1, rep from * to end.
Row 3: P1, *K2tog, rep from * to end. 32 sts.
Row 4: P1, (P2tog) 15 times, P1.
Break yarn and thread through rem 17 sts.
Pull up tight and fasten off securely.
Join back seam.

HANLEY – *Continued from previous page.*

SLEEVES (both alike)

Cast on 48 (48: 50: 52: 52: 54) sts using
4mm (US 6) needles.
Row 1 (RS): P1 (1: 2: 1: 1: 2), *K2, P2, rep
from * to last 3 (3: 0: 3: 3: 0) sts, (K2, P1) 1
(1: 0: 1: 1: 0) times.
Row 2: K1 (1: 2: 1: 1: 2), *P2, K2, rep from *
to last 3 (3: 0: 3: 3: 0) sts, (P2, K1) 1 (1: 0:
1: 1: 0) times.
These 2 rows form rib.
Work in rib for a further 8 rows, inc 1 st at each
end of last row and ending with a WS row.
50 (50: 52: 54: 54: 56) sts.
Change to 4½mm (US 7) needles.
Beg with a K row and working all increases
in same way as back armhole increases, now

work in st st, shaping sides by inc 1 st at each
end of next and foll 0 (3: 4: 4: 7: 8) alt rows,
then on every foll 4th row until there are 108
(112: 116: 120: 124: 128) sts.
Work 6 rows, ending with a **RS** row. (Sleeve
should measure 47 (48: 49: 50: 51: 52) cm.)
Shape top
Place markers at both ends of last row.
Work 7 rows, ending with a WS row.
Cast off.

MAKING UP

Press all pieces with a warm iron over a
damp cloth.
Join right shoulder seam using back stitch
or mattress stitch if preferred.

Neckband

With RS facing and using 3¾mm (US 5)
needles, pick up and knit 12 (12: 12:
13: 13: 13) sts down left side of neck,
50 (52: 52: 52: 52: 52) sts from front,
12 (12: 12: 13: 13: 13) sts up right side
of neck, then 64 (66: 66: 68: 68: 68) sts
from back.
138 (142: 142: 146: 146: 146) sts.
Beg with row 1, work in rib as given for
back for 8 rows, ending with a RS row.
Cast off in rib (on WS).
Join left shoulder and neckband seam.
Matching sleeve markers to top of side
seams, sew sleeves into armholes.
Join side and sleeve seams.

Recommendation

Suitable for the knitter with a little experience
Please see pages 50 & 51 for photographs.

	XS	S	M	L	XL	XXL	
To fit	**81**	**86**	**91**	**97**	**102**	**109**	cm
bust	32	34	36	38	40	43	in

Rowan Big Wool

9	9	10	10	11	12 x 100gm

Photographed in Smoky

Needles

1 pair 9mm (no 00) (US 13) needles
1 pair 10mm (no 000) (US 15) needles
1 pair 12mm (US 17) needles
Cable needle

Buttons – 7

Tension

10 sts and 13 rows to 10 cm measured over
reverse stocking stitch using 10mm (US 15)
needles.

Special abbreviations

C4B = slip next st onto cn and leave at back of
work, K3, then K1 from cn; **C4F** = slip next 3
sts onto cn and leave at front of work, K1, then
K3 from cn; **C6B** = slip next 3 sts onto cn and
leave at back of work, K3, then K3 from cn;
C6F = slip next 3 sts onto cn and leave at front
of work, K3, then K3 from cn; **Cr4L** = slip next
3 sts onto cn and leave at front of work, P1,
then K3 from cn; **Cr4R** = slip next st onto cn
and leave at back of work, K3, then P1 from cn;
cn = cable needle.

TOUGH
Slightly fitted jacket with cables & generous collar

BACK

Cast on 48 (50: 52: 56: 58: 62) sts using
9mm (US 13) needles.
Row 1 (RS): K0 (0: 1: 0: 0: 0), P1 (2: 2: 1: 2:
0), (K2, P2) 2 (2: 2: 3: 3: 4) times, (K3, P2, K2,
P2) 3 times, K3, (P2, K2) 2 (2: 2: 3: 3: 4) times,
P1 (2: 2: 1: 2: 0), K0 (0: 1: 0: 0: 0).
Row 2: P0 (0: 1: 0: 0: 0), K1 (2: 2: 1: 2: 0),
(P2, K2) 2 (2: 2: 3: 3: 4) times, (P3, K2, P2, K2)
3 times, P3, (K2, P2) 2 (2: 2: 3: 3: 4) times, K1
(2: 2: 1: 2: 0), P0 (0: 1: 0: 0: 0).
These 2 rows form rib.
Work in rib for a further 5 rows, ending with
a RS row.
Row 8 (WS): Rib 14 (15: 16: 18: 19: 21),
M1, rib 2, M1, rib 16, M1, rib 2, M1, rib
14 (15: 16: 18: 19: 21).
52 (54: 56: 60: 62: 66) sts.
Change to 10mm (US 15) needles.
Now work in patt, placing cable panels as folls:
Row 1 (RS): P9 (10: 11: 13: 14: 16), work
next 14 sts as row 1 of cable panel A, P6,
work next 14 sts as row 1 of cable panel B,
P9 (10: 11: 13: 14: 16).
Row 2: K9 (10: 11: 13: 14: 16), work next
14 sts as row 2 of cable panel B, K6, work
next 14 sts as row 2 of cable panel A, K9 (10:
11: 13: 14: 16).
These 2 rows set the sts - 2 cable panels with
rev st st between and at sides.
(**Note:** When working cable panels, work rows
1 to 18 **once only** and then rep rows 19 to
46 as required.)
Keeping sts correct as now set and working
appropriate rows of cable panels, cont as folls:
Next row (RS): P3, P2tog, patt to last 5 sts,
P2tog tbl, P3.
Working all side seam decreases as set by
last row, dec 1 st at each end of 4th and
2 foll 4th rows. 44 (46: 48: 52: 54: 58) sts.
Work 9 rows, ending with a WS row.
Next row (RS): P2, M1, patt to last 2 sts,
M1, P2.
Working all side seam increases as set by last
row, inc 1 st at each end of 4th and 3 foll 4th
rows, taking inc sts into rev st st.
54 (56: 58: 62: 64: 68) sts.
Cont straight until back measures 42 (42: 42:
43: 43: 43) cm, ending with a WS row.

Shape armholes

Keeping patt correct, cast off 3 sts at beg
of next 2 rows. 48 (50: 52: 56: 58: 62) sts.
Dec 1 st at each end of next 1 (3: 3: 5: 5: 7)
rows, then on foll 2 (1: 1: 1: 1: 1) alt rows.
42 (42: 44: 44: 46: 46) sts.
Cont straight until armhole measures 18 (19:
20: 20: 21: 22) cm, ending with a WS row.
Shape shoulders and back neck
Next row (RS): Cast off 6 (6: 7: 6: 7: 7) sts,
patt until there are 10 sts on right needle
and turn, leaving rem sts on a holder.
Work each side of neck separately.
Cast off 3 sts at beg of next row.
Cast off rem 7 sts.
With RS facing, rejoin yarn to rem sts, cast off
centre 10 (10: 10: 12: 12: 12) sts, patt to end.
Complete to match first side, reversing
shapings.

LEFT FRONT

Cast on 28 (29: 30: 32: 33: 35) sts using
9mm (US 13) needles.
Row 1 (RS): K0 (0: 1: 0: 0: 0), P1 (2: 2:
1: 2: 0), (K2, P2) 2 (2: 2: 3: 3: 4) times, K3,
P2, K2, P2, K3, P2, K5.
Row 2: K7, P3, K2, P2, K2, P3, (K2, P2)
2 (2: 2: 3: 3: 4) times, K1 (2: 2: 1: 2: 0),
P0 (0: 1: 0: 0: 0).
These 2 rows set the sts - front opening edge
5 sts in g st with all other sts in rib.
Cont as set for a further 5 rows, ending with
a **RS** row.
Row 8 (WS): Patt 12 sts, M1, rib 2, M1, rib 14
(15: 16: 18: 19: 21). 30 (31: 32: 34: 35: 37) sts.
Change to 10mm (US 15) needles.
Now work in patt, placing cable panel as folls:
Row 1 (RS): P9 (10: 11: 13: 14: 16), work
next 14 sts as row 1 of cable panel A, P2, K5.
Row 2: K7, work next 14 sts as row 2 of cable
panel A, K9 (10: 11: 13: 14: 16).
These 2 rows set the sts - cable panel A with
rev st st each side and front opening edge
5 sts still in g st.
Keeping sts correct as now set, working
appropriate rows of cable panel and all side
seam shaping as given for back, cont as folls:
Dec 1 st at beg of next and 3 foll 4th rows.
26 (27: 28: 30: 31: 33) sts.
Work 9 rows, ending with a WS row.

Inc 1 st at beg of next and 4 foll 4th rows, taking inc sts into rev st st.
31 (32: 33: 35: 36: 38) sts.
Cont straight until left front matches back to start of armhole shaping, ending with a WS row.

Shape armhole
Keeping patt correct, cast off 3 sts at beg of next row. 28 (29: 30: 32: 33: 35) sts.
Work 1 row.
Dec 1 st at armhole edge of next 1 (3: 3: 5: 5: 7) rows, then on foll 2 (1: 1: 1: 1: 1) alt rows. 25 (25: 26: 26: 27: 27) sts.
Cont straight until 10 (10: 10: 12: 12: 12) rows less have been worked than on back to start of shoulder shaping, ending with a WS row.

Shape front neck
Next row (RS): Patt 19 (19: 20: 20: 21: 21) sts and turn, leaving rem 6 sts on a holder.
Keeping patt correct, dec 1 st at neck edge of next 4 rows, then on foll 2 (2: 2: 3: 3: 3) alt rows.
13 (13: 14: 13: 14: 14) sts.
Work 1 row, ending with a WS row.
Shape shoulder
Cast off 6 (6: 7: 6: 7: 7) sts at beg of next row.
Work 1 row.
Cast off rem 7 sts.
Mark positions for 6 buttons along left front opening edge - first to come in row 11, last to come in neck shaping row, and rem 4 buttons evenly spaced between.

RIGHT FRONT
Cast on 28 (29: 30: 32: 33: 35) sts using 9mm (US 13) needles.
Row 1 (RS): K5, P2, K3, P2, K2, P2, K3, (P2, K2) 2 (2: 2: 3: 3: 4) times, P1 (2: 2: 1: 2: 0), K0 (0: 1: 0: 0: 0).
Row 2: P0 (0: 1: 0: 0: 0), K1 (2: 2: 1: 2: 0), (P2, K2) 2 (2: 2: 3: 3: 4) times, P3, K2, P2, K2, P3, K7.
These 2 rows set the sts - front opening edge 5 sts in g st with all other sts in rib.
Cont as set for a further 5 rows, ending with a **RS** row.
Row 8 (WS): Rib 14 (15: 16: 18: 19: 21), M1, rib 2, M1, patt 12 sts.
30 (31: 32: 34: 35: 37) sts.
Change to 10mm (US 15) needles.
Now work in patt, placing cable panel as folls:
Row 1 (RS): K5, P2, work next 14 sts as row 1 of cable panel B, P9 (10: 11: 13: 14: 16).
Row 2: K9 (10: 11: 13: 14: 16), work next 14 sts as row 2 of cable panel B, K7.
These 2 rows set the sts - cable panel B with rev st st each side and front opening edge 5 sts still in g st.
Keeping sts correct as now set, working appropriate rows of cable panel and all side seam shaping as given for back, cont as folls:
Next row (buttonhole row) (RS): K1, K2tog tbl, yfwd (to make a buttonhole), patt to last 5 sts, P2tog tbl, P3.
Working a further 4 buttonholes in this way and noting that no further reference will be made to buttonholes, complete to match left front, reversing shapings and working first row of neck shaping as folls:
Shape front neck
Next row (RS): K1, K2tog tbl, yfwd (to make 6th buttonhole), K2, P1 and slip these 6 sts onto another holder, patt to end.
19 (19: 20: 20: 21: 21) sts.

SLEEVES (both alike)
Cast on 26 (26: 28: 28: 30: 30) sts using 9mm (US 13) needles.
Row 1 (RS): P0 (0: 1: 1: 2: 2), K2, *P2, K2, rep from * to last 0 (0: 1: 1: 2: 2) sts, P0 (0: 1: 1: 2: 2).
Row 2: K0 (0: 1: 1: 2: 2), P2, *K2, P2, rep from * to last 0 (0: 1: 1: 2: 2) sts, K0 (0: 1: 1: 2: 2).
These 2 rows form rib.
Cont in rib, inc 1 st at each end of 11th row.
28 (28: 30: 30: 32: 32) sts.
Work a further 7 rows, inc 1 st at centre of last row and ending with a WS row.
29 (29: 31: 31: 33: 33) sts.

Cable Panel B

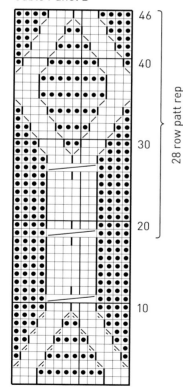

46
40
30
20
10

28 row patt rep

Cable Panel A

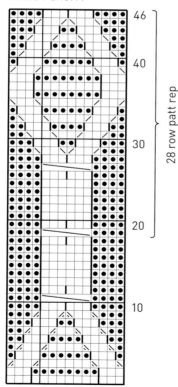

46
40
30
20
10

28 row patt rep

KEY
☐	K on RS, P on WS
⊡	P on RS, K on WS
▱ C6B	
▱ C6F	

C4B	
C4F	
Cr4R	
Cr4L	

Change to 10mm (US 15) needles.
Beg with a P row and working all increases
in same way as side seam increases, now
work in rev st st, shaping sides by inc 1 st
at each end of 5th and 2 foll 14th rows.
35 (35: 37: 37: 39: 39) sts.
Cont straight until sleeve measures
47 (48: 49: 50: 51: 52) cm, ending
with a WS row.

Shape top
Cast off 3 sts at beg of next 2 rows.
29 (29: 31: 31: 33: 33) sts.
Dec 1 st at each end of next and
2 foll 4th rows.
23 (23: 25: 25: 27: 27) sts.
Work 1 row, ending with a WS row.
Dec 1 st at each end of next and every foll
alt row to 19 sts, then on foll 3 rows,
ending with a WS row.
Cast off rem 13 sts.

MAKING UP
Press all pieces with a warm iron over
a damp cloth.
Join both shoulder seams using back stitch
or mattress stitch if preferred.

Collar
With RS facing and using 10mm (US 15)
needles, slip 6 sts on right front holder onto
right needle, rejoin yarn and pick up and knit
10 (10: 10: 13: 13: 13) sts up right side of
neck, 16 (16: 16: 18: 18: 18) sts from back,
and 10 (10: 10: 13: 13: 13) sts down left side
of neck, then patt 6 sts on left front holder.
48 (48: 48: 56: 56: 56) sts.
Row 1 (RS of collar, WS of body): K7, *P2,
K2, rep from * to last 5 sts, K5.
Row 2: K5, *P2, K2, rep from * to last 3 sts, K3.
These 2 rows set the sts - 5 sts at each end
of rows still in g st with all other sts in rib.
Cont as set for a further 5 rows, ending with
WS of collar (RS of body) facing for next row.
Row 8 (WS of collar): K1, K2tog tbl, yfwd (to
make 7th buttonhole), patt to end.
Work 2 rows.
Row 11 (RS of collar): K6, M1, K1, *P2, K1,
M1, K1, rep from * to last 5 sts, K5.
58 (58: 58: 68: 68: 68) sts.
Row 12: K5, *P3, K2, rep from * to last 3 sts, K3.
Row 13: K8, *P2, K3, rep from * to last 5 sts, K5.
Rep last 2 rows 6 times more.
Change to 12mm (US 17) needles.
Work a further 6 rows.
Cast off in patt (on **WS** of collar).
Join side seams. Join sleeve seams. Sew
sleeves into armholes. Sew on buttons.

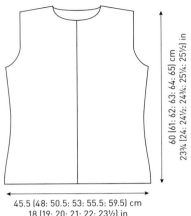

45.5 (48: 50.5: 53: 55.5: 59.5) cm
18 (19: 20: 21: 22: 23½) in

60 (61: 62: 63: 64: 65) cm
23¾ (24: 24½: 24¾: 25¼: 25½) in

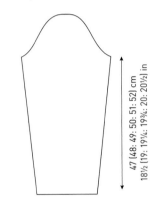

47 (48: 49: 50: 51: 52) cm
18½ (19: 19¼: 19¾: 20: 20½) in

BRAD

A-line cardigan worked in an open fabric

Recommendation

Suitable for the knitter with a little experience
Please see pages 52 & 53 for photographs.

	XS	S	M	L	XL	XXL	
To fit	81	86	91	97	102	109	cm
bust	32	34	36	38	40	43	in

Rowan by Amy Butler Sweet Harmony

6   7   7   8   8   9 x100gm

Photographed in Cinder

Needles

1 pair 8mm (no 0) (US 11) needles
1 pair 15mm (US 19) needles

Tension

7 sts and 10½ rows to 10 cm measured over
pattern using a combination of 8mm (US 11)
and 15mm (US 19) needles.

BACK

Cast on 39 (41: 43: 45: 47: 49) sts using
15mm (US 19) needles.
Row 1 (RS): Using a 8mm (US 11) needle,
purl.
Row 2: Using a 15mm (US 19) needle, knit.
These 2 rows form patt.
Work in patt for a further 12 rows, ending
with a WS row.
Row 15 (RS): P2, P2tog, P to last 4 sts,
P2tog tbl, P2.
Working all side seam decreases as set by
last row, dec 1 st at each end of 14th and foll
14th row. 33 (35: 37: 39: 41: 43) sts.
Cont straight until back measures 55 (55: 55:
56: 56: 56) cm, ending with a WS row.
Shape armholes
Cast off 2 sts at beg of next 2 rows.
29 (31: 33: 35: 37: 39) sts.
Dec 1 st at each end of next 1 (1: 1: 1: 1: 3)
rows, then on foll 1 (2: 2: 3: 3: 2) alt rows.
25 (25: 27: 27: 29: 29) sts.
Cont straight until armhole measures 19 (20:
21: 21: 22: 23) cm, ending with a WS row.
Shape shoulders
Cast off 3 (3: 4: 3: 4: 4) sts at beg of next
2 rows, then 4 sts at beg of foll row.
Cast off all rem sts (on **WS**), placing marker
after 4th cast-off st (to denote left shoulder
neck point).

LEFT FRONT

Cast on 25 (26: 27: 28: 29: 30) sts using
15mm (US 19) needles.
Row 1 (RS): Using a 8mm (US 11) needle,
P to last 2 sts, K2.
Row 2: Using a 15mm (US 19) needle, knit.
These 2 rows form patt.
Work in patt for a further 12 rows, ending
with a WS row.
Working all side seam decreases as set
by back, dec 1 st at beg of next and 2 foll
14th rows. 22 (23: 24: 25: 26: 27) sts.
Cont straight until left front matches back
to start of armhole shaping, ending with
a WS row.
Shape armhole
Cast off 2 sts at beg of next row.
20 (21: 22: 23: 24: 25) sts.
Work 1 row.

Dec 1 st at armhole edge of next 1 (1: 1:
1: 1: 3) rows, then on foll 1 (2: 2: 3: 3: 2)
alt rows. 18 (18: 19: 19: 20: 20) sts.
Cont straight until left front matches back to
start of shoulder shaping, ending with a WS row.
Shape shoulder
Cast off 3 (3: 4: 3: 4: 4) sts at beg of next row,
then 4 sts at beg of foll alt row.
11 (11: 11: 12: 12: 12) sts.
Cont in patt on these sts for a further 9 (9: 9:
11: 11: 11) rows (for back neck border
extension), ending with a WS row.
Cast off 5 (5: 5: 6: 6: 6) sts at beg of next row.
Work 1 row.
Cast off rem 6 sts.

RIGHT FRONT

Cast on 25 (26: 27: 28: 29: 30) sts using
15mm (US 19) needles.
Row 1 (RS): Using a 8mm (US 11) needle,
K2, P to end.
Row 2: Using a 15mm (US 19) needle, knit.
These 2 rows form patt.
Work in patt for a further 12 rows, ending
with a WS row.
Working all side seam decreases as set
by back, dec 1 st at end of next and 2 foll
14th rows. 22 (23: 24: 25: 26: 27) sts.
Complete to match left front, rev shapings.

SLEEVES (both alike)

Cast on 18 (18: 20: 20: 20: 22) sts using
15mm (US 19) needles.
Beg with a P row using 8mm (US 11) needle
and working all increases in same way as side
seam increases, work in patt as given for back,
shaping sides by inc 1 st at each end of 15th
and 3 (2: 2: 1: 1: 0) foll 10th rows, then on
0 (1: 1: 2: 2: 3) foll 12th rows.
26 (26: 28: 28: 28: 30) sts.
Cont straight until sleeve measures 47 (48: 49:
50: 51: 52) cm, ending with a WS row.
Shape top
Cast off 2 sts at beg of next 2 rows.
22 (22: 24: 24: 24: 26) sts.
Dec 1 st at each end of next and 2 foll 4th
rows, then on foll 2 (2: 1: 1: 3: 2) alt rows,
then on foll 1 (1: 3: 3: 1: 3) rows, ending
with a WS row. Cast off rem 10 sts.

Continued on next page...

Recommendation

Suitable for the novice knitter
Please see page 44 for photograph.

	XS	S	M	L	XL	XXL	
To fit	**81**	**86**	**91**	**97**	**102**	**109**	**cm**
bust	32	34	36	38	40	43	in

Rowan Cocoon

	8	8	9	9	10	10 x100gm

Photographed in Scree

Needles

1 pair 5mm (no 6) (US 8) needles
1 pair 6mm (no 4) (US 10) needles
1 pair 7mm (no 2) (US 10½ /11) needles

Tension

15 sts and 20 rows to 10 cm measured over
pattern using 7mm (US 10½) needles.

BARON
Belted poncho worked in double moss stitch

BACK

Cast on 87 (91: 95: 99: 103: 109) sts using
7mm (US 10½ /11) needles.
Row 1 (RS): K5 (5: 6: 6: 7: 7), *P1, K1,
rep from * to last 6 (6: 7: 7: 8: 8) sts, P1,
K5 (5: 6: 6: 7: 7).
Row 2: K7 (7: 8: 8: 9: 9), *P1, K1, rep from *
to last 6 (6: 7: 7: 8: 8) sts, K6 (6: 7: 7: 8: 8).
Row 3: K5 (5: 6: 6: 7: 7), P2, *K1, P1,
rep from * to last 6 (6: 7: 7: 8: 8) sts, P1,
K5 (5: 6: 6: 7: 7).
Row 4: K6 (6: 7: 7: 8: 8), P1, *K1, P1,
rep from * to last 6 (6: 7: 7: 8: 8) sts,
K6 (6: 7: 7: 8: 8).
These 4 rows form patt.
Cont in patt until back measures 27 (28: 29:
29: 30: 31) cm, ending with a WS row.
Next row (RS): Patt 20 (21: 23: 24: 26: 29)
sts, K5, patt 37 (39: 39: 41: 41: 41) sts, K5,
patt 20 (21: 23: 24: 26: 29) sts.
Rep last row twice more, ending with
a RS row.

Divide for belt slit openings

Place markers on 11th (12th: 13th: 13th:
14th: 16th) sts in from both ends of last row.
Next row (WS): Patt 20 (21: 23: 24: 26: 29) sts,
K1, K2tog and turn, leaving rem sts on a holder.

Keeping sts correct as set, work 16 rows on
these 22 (23: 25: 26: 28: 31) sts only for
first side section, ending with a WS row.
Break yarn and leave sts on a 2nd holder.
With **WS** facing, rejoin yarn to sts on first
holder, K2, patt 37 (39: 39: 41: 41: 41) sts,
K2 and turn, leaving rem sts on a holder.
Keeping sts correct as set, work 16 rows on
these 41 (43: 43: 45: 45: 45) sts only for
centre section, ending with a WS row.
Break yarn and leave sts on a 3rd holder.
With **WS** facing, rejoin yarn to sts on first
holder, K2tog tbl, K1, patt to end.
Keeping sts correct as set, work 16 rows on
these 22 (23: 25: 26: 28: 31) sts only for
second side section, ending with a WS row.

Join sections

Next row (RS): Patt to last st of second side
section, inc in last st, patt to last st of centre
section, inc in last st, patt to end of sts of first
side section.
87 (91: 95: 99: 103: 109) sts.
Place markers on 11th (12th: 13th: 13th:
14th: 16th) sts in from both ends of last row.
Keeping sts correct as set, work a further
4 rows, ending with a RS row.
Beg with patt row 2, now work all sts in patt
and cont as folls:

BRAD – *Continued from previous page.*

MAKING UP

Press all pieces with a warm iron over a damp
cloth.
Join both shoulder seams using back stitch or
mattress stitch if preferred. Join cast-off ends
of back neck border extensions, then sew one
edge to back neck. Join side seams.
Join sleeve seams.
Sew sleeves into armholes.

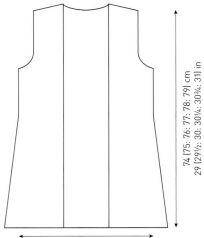

74 (75: 76: 77: 78: 79) cm
29 (29½: 30: 30¼: 30¾: 31) in

47 (50: 53: 55.5: 58.5: 61.5) cm
18½ (19½: 20¾: 21¾: 23: 24¼) in

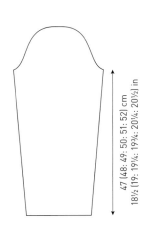

47 (48: 49: 50: 51: 52) cm
18½ (19: 19¼: 19¾: 20¼: 20½) in

Cont straight until back measures 65 (66: 67: 68: 69: 70) cm, ending with a WS row.

Shape shoulders and back neck
Cast off 9 (9: 10: 10: 11: 12) sts at beg of next 2 rows. 69 (73: 75: 79: 81: 85) sts.

Next row (RS): Cast off 9 (9: 10: 10: 11: 12) sts, patt until there are 13 (14: 14: 15: 15: 16) sts on right needle and turn, leaving rem sts on a holder.
Work each side of neck separately.
Cast off 4 sts at beg of next row.
Cast off rem 9 (10: 10: 11: 11: 12) sts.
With RS facing, rejoin yarn to rem sts, cast off centre 25 (27: 27: 29: 29: 29) sts, patt to end.
Complete to match first side, reversing shapings.

FRONT
Work as given for back until 4 (4: 4: 6: 6: 6) rows less have been worked than on back to start of shoulder shaping, ending with a WS row.

Shape front neck
Next row (RS): Patt 31 (32: 34: 36: 38: 41) sts and turn, leaving rem sts on a holder.
Work each side of neck separately.
Dec 1 st at neck edge of next 3 (3: 3: 4: 4: 4) rows. 28 (29: 31: 32: 34: 37) sts.
Work 0 (0: 0: 1: 1: 1) row, ending with a WS row.

Shape shoulder
Cast off 9 (9: 10: 10: 11: 12) sts at beg of next and foll alt row **and at same time** dec 1 st at neck edge of next row.
Work 1 row.
Cast off rem 9 (10: 10: 11: 11: 12) sts.
With RS facing, rejoin yarn to rem sts, cast off centre 25 (27: 27: 27: 27: 27) sts, patt to end.
Complete to match first side, reversing shapings.

MAKING UP
Press all pieces with a warm iron over a damp cloth.
Join right shoulder seam using back stitch or mattress stitch if preferred.

Neckband
With RS facing and using 6mm (US 10) needles, pick up and knit 8 (8: 8: 10: 10: 10) sts down left side of neck, 25 (27: 27: 27: 27: 27) sts from front, 8 (8: 8: 10: 10: 10) sts up right side of neck, then 33 (35: 35: 37: 37: 37) sts from back.
74 (78: 78: 84: 84: 84) sts.
Beg with a K row, work in rev st st for 4 rows, ending with a **RS** row.
Cast off knitwise (on **WS**).

Join left shoulder and neckband seam.
Lay garment flat so that markers match.
Using photograph as a guide, sew back and front together between markers.

Belt
Cast on 12 sts using 5mm (US 8) needles.
Work in g st until belt measures 155 (160: 165: 170: 175: 180) cm.
Cast off.
Thread belt through belt slit openings and tie as in photograph.

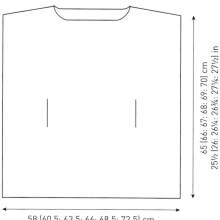

58 (60.5: 63.5: 66: 68.5: 72.5) cm
22¾ (23¾: 25: 26: 27: 28½) in

65 (66: 67: 68: 69: 70) cm
25½ (26: 26¼: 26¾: 27¼: 27½) in

Recommendation

Suitable for the novice knitter

Please see pages 54, 55 & 57 for photographs.

	XS	S	M	L	XL	XXL	
To fit	**81**	**86**	**91**	**97**	**102**	**109**	**cm**
bust	32	34	36	38	40	43	in

Rowan Alpaca Cotton

| A | 4 | 4 | 5 | 5 | 6 | 7 | x 50gm |
| B | 4 | 4 | 5 | 5 | 6 | 7 | x 50gm |

Photographed in Storm and Thunder

Needles

1 pair 7mm (no 2) (US 10½/11) needles

Tension

13 sts and 20 rows to 10 cm measured over
stocking stitch using 7mm (US 10½/11)
needles.

RUMBLE
Striped classic sweater with square set in sleeves

BACK

Cast on 63 (67: 71: 73: 77: 81) sts using
7mm (US 10½/11) needles and yarn A.
Beg with a K row, work in st st for 8 rows,
ending with a WS row.
Join in yarn B and now work in striped
st st as folls:
Rows 1 to 6: Using yarn B.
Rows 7 to 12: Using yarn A.
These 12 rows form striped st st.
Cont in striped st st until back measures
40 (40: 40: 41: 41: 41) cm, end with a WS row.
Shape armholes
Keeping stripes correct, cast off 4 sts at beg
of next 2 rows. 55 (59: 63: 65: 69: 73) sts.
Work 6 rows, ending with a WS row.
Next row (RS): K3, M1, K to last 3 sts, M1, K3.
Working all increases as set by last row, inc 1
st at each end of 8th (8th: 10th: 10th: 10th:
10th) and 1 (0: 2: 2: 1: 0) foll 8th (8th: 10th:
10th: 10th: 10th) rows, then on 1 (2: -: -: 1: 2)
foll 10th (10th: -: -: 12th: 12th) rows.
63 (67: 71: 73: 77: 81) sts.
Cont straight until armhole measures 23 (24:
25: 25: 26: 27) cm, ending with a WS row.
Shape shoulders and back neck
Keeping stripes correct, cast off 5 (5: 6: 6: 6: 7)
sts at beg of next 2 rows.
53 (57: 59: 61: 65: 67) sts.
Next row (RS): Cast off 5 (5: 6: 6: 6: 7) sts,
K until there are 8 (9: 9: 9: 11: 11) sts on right
needle and turn, leaving rem sts on a holder.
Work each side of neck separately.
Cast off 4 sts at beg of next row.
Cast off rem 4 (5: 5: 5: 7: 7) sts.
With RS facing, rejoin appropriate yarn to rem
sts, cast off centre 27 (29: 29: 31: 31: 31) sts,
K to end.
Complete to match first side, reversing
shapings.

FRONT

Work as given for back until 4 (4: 4: 6: 6: 6)
rows less have been worked than on back
to start of shoulder shaping, ending with
a WS row.
Shape front neck
Next row (RS): K17 (18: 20: 21: 23: 25) and
turn, leaving rem sts on a holder.
Work each side of neck separately.

Keeping stripes correct, dec 1 st at neck
edge of next 2 rows, then on foll 0 (0: 0:
1: 1: 1) alt rows. 15 (16: 18: 18: 20: 22) sts.
Work 1 row, ending with a WS row.
Shape shoulder
Cast off 5 (5: 6: 6: 6: 7) sts at beg of next and
foll alt row **and at same time** dec 1 st at neck
edge of next row.
Work 1 row.
Cast off rem 4 (5: 5: 5: 7: 7) sts.
With RS facing, rejoin appropriate yarn to rem
sts, cast off centre 29 (31: 31: 31: 31: 31) sts,
K to end.
Complete to match first side, rev shapings.

SLEEVES (both alike)

Cast on 29 (31: 33: 33: 35: 37) sts using
7mm (US 10½/11) needles and yarn A.
Beg with a K row and working all increases in
same way as back armhole increases, work in
st st for 8 rows, inc 1 st at each end of 7th of
these rows and ending with a WS row.
31 (33: 35: 35: 37: 39) sts.
Join in yarn B.
Beg with 6 rows using yarn B, now work in
striped st st as given for back as folls:
Inc 1 st at each end of 3rd and 1 (3: 2: 1:
0: 2) foll 4th rows, then on every foll 6th row
until there are 59 (63: 65: 65: 67: 71) sts.
Work 7 rows, ending with a WS row. (Sleeve
should measure 47 (48: 49: 50: 51: 52) cm.)
Shape top
Place markers at both ends of last row.
Work 6 rows, ending with a WS row.
Cast off **loosely**.

MAKING UP

Press all pieces with a warm iron over a
damp cloth.
Join right shoulder seam using back stitch
or mattress stitch if preferred.
Neckband
With RS facing, using 7mm (US 10½/11)
needles and yarn A, pick up and knit 8 (8:
8: 10: 10: 10) sts down left side of neck,
29 (31: 31: 31: 31: 31) sts from front, 8
(8: 8: 10: 10: 10) sts up right side of neck,
then 35 (37: 37: 39: 39: 39) sts from back.
80 (84: 84: 90: 90: 90) sts.

Continued on next page...

CARTER
Over sized double fabric scarf

SCARF
Cast on 71 sts using 10mm (US 15) needles.
Row 1 (RS): K1, *slip next st purlwise with yarn at back (WS) of work, K1, rep from * to end.
Row 2: K1, *P1, K1, rep from * to end.
These 2 rows form patt.
Cont in patt until scarf measures 230 cm, ending with a **RS** row.
Cast off **firmly** in patt (on **WS**).

Recommendation
Suitable for the novice knitter
Please see pages 40 & 41 for photographs.

Rowan Alpaca Cotton
6   x 50gm
Photographed in Storm

Needles
1 pair 10mm (no 000) (US 15) needles

Tension
17 sts and 20 rows to 10 cm measured over pattern using 10mm (US 15) needles.

Finished size
Completed scarf measures 42 cm (16½ ins) wide and 230 cm (90½ ins) long.

RUMBLE – *Continued from previous page.*

Beg with a P row, work in st st as folls:
Using yarn A, work 5 rows.
Join in yarn B.
Using yarn B, work 6 rows.
Using yarn A, work 6 rows.
Using yarn B, work 5 rows, ending with a **RS** row.
Cast off **loosely knitwise** (on **WS**).
Join left shoulder and neckband seam.
Matching sleeve markers to top of side seams, sew sleeves into armholes.
Join side and sleeve seams.

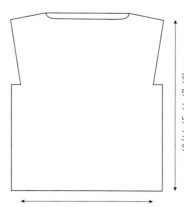

63 (64: 65: 66: 67: 68) cm
24¾ (25¼: 25½: 26: 26½: 26¾) in

48.5 (51.5: 54: 56: 59: 62.5) cm
19 (20: 2¼: 22: 23: 24½) in

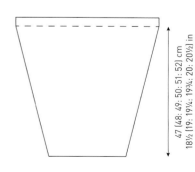

47 (48: 49: 50: 51: 52) cm
18½ (19: 19¼: 19¾: 20: 20½) in

DERWIN

A-line sweater with cables set in a ribbed fabric

Recommendation

Suitable for the knitter with a little experience
Please see pages 42, 43 & 45 for photographs.

	XS	S	M	L	XL	XXL	
To fit	81	86	91	97	102	109	cm
bust	32	34	36	38	40	43	in

Rowan Baby Alpaca DK

	12	13	14	15	16	18	x50gm

Photographed in Southdown

Needles

1 pair 3¼mm (no 10) (US 3) needles
1 pair 3¾mm (no 9) (US 5) needles
Cable needle

Tension

23 sts and 35 rows to 10 cm measured over
textured pattern using 3¾mm (US 5) needles.

Special abbreviations

C4B = slip next 2 sts onto cn and leave at back
of work, K2, then K2 from cn; **C4F** = slip next 2
sts onto cn and leave at front of work, K2, then
K2 from cn; **C6B** = slip next 3 sts onto cn and
leave at back of work, K3, then K3 from cn;
C6F = slip next 3 sts onto cn and leave at front
of work, K3, then K3 from cn; **C8B** = slip next
4 sts onto cn and leave at back of work, K4,
then K4 from cn; **C8F** = slip next 4 sts onto cn
and leave at front of work, K4, then K4 from cn;
cn = cable needle.

BACK and FRONT (both alike)

Cast on 131 (137: 143: 149: 155: 163) sts
using 3¾mm (US 5) needles.
Row 1 (RS): K0 (2: 1: 0: 0: 0), P0 (1: 1:
1: 0: 0), (K3, P1) 5 (5: 6: 7: 8: 9) times,
*(K1, inc in next st, K1) twice, P1, (K1, inc
in next st, K1) twice, P1, (K3, P1) 3 times,
rep from * twice more, (K1, inc in next st,
K1) twice, P1, (K1, inc in next st, K1) twice,
(P1, K3) 5 (5: 6: 7: 8: 9) times, P0 (1: 1:
1: 0: 0), K0 (2: 1: 0: 0: 0).
147 (153: 159: 165: 171: 179) sts.
Now work in cable patt as folls:
Row 2 (WS): K1 (0: 0: 2: 1: 1), P1 (1: 0:
1: 1: 1), (K3, P1) 4 (5: 6: 6: 7: 8) times, K2,
*P8, K1, P8, K2, (P1, K3) twice, P1, K2, rep
from * twice more, P8, K1, P8, K2, (P1, K3)
4 (5: 6: 6: 7: 8) times, P1 (1: 0: 1: 1: 1),
K1 (0: 0: 2: 1: 1).
Row 3: K0 (2: 1: 0: 0: 0), P0 (1: 1: 1: 0: 0),
(K3, P1) 5 (5: 6: 7: 8: 9) times, *(K8, P1),
twice, (K3, P1) 3 times, rep from * twice
more, K8, P1, K8, (P1, K3) 5 (5: 6: 7: 8: 9)
times, P0 (1: 1: 1: 0: 0), K0 (2: 1: 0: 0: 0).
Rows 4 to 11: As rows 2 and 3, 4 times.
Row 12: As row 2.
Row 13: K0 (2: 1: 0: 0: 0), P0 (1: 1: 1: 0:
0), (K3, P1) 5 (5: 6: 7: 8: 9) times, *C8B,
P1, C8F, P1, (K3, P1) 3 times, rep from *
twice more, C8B, P1, C8F, (P1, K3) 5 (5: 6:
7: 8: 9) times, P0 (1: 1: 1: 0: 0), K0 (2: 1:
0: 0: 0).
Rows 14 to 19: As rows 2 and 3, 3 times.
Rows 2 to 19 form cable patt.
Work in patt for a further 31 rows, ending
with a WS row.
Row 51 (RS): K0 (2: 1: 0: 0: 0), P0 (1: 1:
1: 0: 0), (K3, P1) 5 (5: 6: 7: 8: 9) times,
*slip next 4 sts onto cn and leave at back
of work, K2, K2tog, then K2tog, K2 from cn,
P1, slip next 4 sts onto cn and leave
at front of work, K2, K2tog, then K2tog,
K2 from cn, P1, (K3, P1) 3 times, rep from
* twice more, slip next 4 sts onto cn and
leave at back of work, K2, K2tog, then
K2tog, K2 from cn, P1, slip next 4 sts onto
cn and leave at front of work, K2, K2tog,
then K2tog, K2 from cn, (P1, K3) 5 (5: 6: 7:
8: 9) times, P0 (1: 1: 1: 0: 0), K0 (2: 1: 0:
0: 0). 131 (137: 143: 149: 155: 163) sts.

Now working cables on every 16th row instead
of every 18th row, C6B instead of C8B and C6F
instead of C8F, cont in patt for a further 45
rows, ending with a WS row.
Row 97 (RS): K0 (2: 1: 0: 0: 0), P0 (1: 1:
1: 0: 0), (K3, P1) 5 (5: 6: 7: 8: 9) times,
*slip next 3 sts onto cn and leave at back
of work, K1, K2tog, then K2tog, K1 from
cn, P1, slip next 3 sts onto cn and leave at
front of work, K1, K2tog, then K2tog, K1
from cn, P1, (K3, P1)
3 times, rep from * twice more, slip next
3 sts onto cn and leave at back of work, K1,
K2tog, then K2tog, K1 from cn, P1, slip next
3 sts onto cn and leave at front of work,
K1, K2tog, then K2tog, K1 from cn, (P1, K3)
5 (5: 6: 7: 8: 9) times, P0 (1: 1: 1: 0: 0),
K0 (2: 1: 0: 0: 0).
115 (121: 127: 133: 139: 147) sts.
Now working cables on every 12th row
instead of every 16th row, C4B instead of
C6B and C4F instead of C6F, cont in patt
as now set as folls:
Cont straight until work measures 37 (37:
37: 38: 38: 38) cm, ending with a WS row.
Shape armholes
Keeping patt correct, cast off 4 (5: 5: 6: 6: 7)
sts at beg of next 2 rows.
107 (111: 117: 121: 127: 133) sts.
Dec 1 st at each end of next 7 (7: 9: 9: 11: 11)
rows, then on foll 2 (3: 3: 4: 4: 5) alt rows, then
on foll 4th row. 87 (89: 91: 93: 95: 99) sts.
Cont straight until armhole measures 14 (15:
16: 16: 17: 18) cm, ending with a WS row.
Shape neck
Next row (RS): Patt 18 (18: 19: 19: 20: 22)
sts and turn, leaving rem sts on a holder.
Work each side of neck separately.
Keeping patt correct, dec 1 st at neck edge
of next 4 rows, then on foll 2 alt rows.
12 (12: 13: 13: 14: 16) sts.
Work 3 rows, ending with RS facing for next row.
Shape shoulder
Cast off 6 (6: 6: 6: 7: 8) sts at beg of next row.
Work 1 row.
Cast off rem 6 (6: 7: 7: 7: 8) sts.
With RS facing, rejoin yarn to rem sts, cast off
centre 51 (53: 53: 55: 55: 55) sts, patt to end.
Complete to match first side, reversing
shapings.

SLEEVES (both alike)

Cast on 51 (51: 53: 55: 55: 57) sts using
3¼mm (US 3) needles.

Row 1 (RS): K0 (0: 0: 1: 1: 2), P0 (0: 1: 1:
1: 1), *K3, P1, rep from * to last 3 (3: 0: 1:
1: 2) sts, K3 (3: 0: 1: 1: 2).

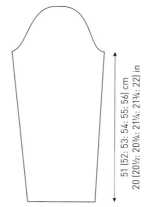

134 (138: 138: 142: 142: 142) sts.
Starting with a K row, work in rev st st for
4 rows, ending with a **RS** row.
Cast off knitwise (on **WS**).
Join left shoulder and neckband seam.
Join side seams.
Join sleeve seams.
Sew sleeves into armholes.

55 (56: 57: 58: 59: 60] cm
21½ (22: 22½: 22¾: 23¼: 23¾) in

43 (45.5: 48: 50.5: 53: 57] cm
17 (18: 19: 20: 21: 22½) in

51 (52: 53: 54: 55: 56] cm
20 (20½: 20¾: 21¼: 21¾: 22) in

INFORMATION

A guide to assist with techniques & finishing touches

TENSION

Achieving the correct tension has to be one of the most important elements in producing a beautiful, well fitting knitted garment.

The tension controls the size and shape of your finished piece and any variation to either stitches or rows, however slight, will affect your work and change the fit completely.

To avoid any disappointment, we would always recommend that you knit a tension square in the yarn and stitch given in the pattern, working perhaps four or five more stitches and rows than those given in the tension note.

When counting the tension, place your knitting on a flat surface and mark out a 10cm square with pins. Count the stitches between the pins. If you have too many stitches to 10cm your knitting it too tight, try again using thicker needles, if you have too few stitches to 10cm your knitting is too loose, so try again using finer needles. Please note, if you are unable to achieve the correct stitches and rows required, the stitches are more crucial as many patterns are knitted to length. Keep an eye on your tension during knitting, especially if you're going back to work which has been put to one side for any length of time.

SIZING

The instructions are given for the smallest size. Where they vary, work the figures in brackets for the larger sizes. One set of figures refers to all sizes. The size diagram with each pattern will help you decide which size to knit. The measurements given on the size diagram are the actual size your garment should be when completed.

Measurements will vary from design to design because the necessary ease allowances have been made in each pattern to give your garment the correct fit, i.e. a loose fitting garment will be several cm wider than a neat fitted one, a snug fitting garment may have no ease at all.

CHART NOTE

Some of our patterns include a chart. Each square on a chart represent a stitch and each line of squares a row of knitting.

When working from a chart, unless otherwise stated, read odd rows (RS) from right to left and even rows (WS) from left to right. The key alongside each chart indicates how each stitch is worked.

FINISHING INSTRUCTIONS

It is the pressing and finishing which will transform your knitted pieces into a garment to be proud of.

Pressing

Darn in ends neatly along the selvage edge. Follow closely any special instructions given on the pattern or ball band and always take great care not to over press your work. Block out your knitting on a pressing or ironing board, easing into shape, and unless otherwise states, press each piece using a warm iron over a damp cloth.

Tip: Attention should be given to ribs/edgings; if the garment is close fitting – steam the ribs gently so that the stitches fill out but stay elastic. Alternatively if the garment is to hang straight then steam out to the correct shape.

Tip: Take special care to press the selvages, as this will make sewing up both easier and neater.

CONSTRUCTION
Stitching together

When stitching the pieces together, remember to match areas of pattern very carefully where they meet.

Use a stitch such as back stitch or mattress stitch for all main knitting seams and join all ribs and neckband with mattress stitch, unless otherwise stated.

Take extra care when stitching the edgings and collars around the back neck of a garment.

They control the width of the back neck, and if too wide the garment will be ill fitting and drop off the shoulder. Knit back neck edgings only to the length stated in the pattern, even stretching it slightly if for example, you are working in garter or horizontal rib stitch. Stitch edgings/collars firmly into place using a back stitch seam, easing-in the back neck to fit the collar/edging rather than stretching the collar/edging to fit the back neck.

Set-in sleeves: Join side and sleeve seams. Place centre of cast off edge of sleeve to shoulder seams. Set in sleeve, easing sleeve head into armhole.

Square set in sleeves: Set the sleeve top into armhole, the straight sides at top of sleeve to form a neat right-angle to cast off stitches at armhole on back and front.

CARE INSTRUCTIONS
Yarns

Follow the care instructions printed on each individual ball band. Where different yarns are used in the same garment, follow the care instructions for the more delicate one.

Buttons

We recommend that buttons are removed if your garment is to be machine washed.

CROCHET

We are aware that crochet terminology varies from country to country. Please note we have used the English style in this publication.

Crochet abbreviations

ch	chain
ss	slip stitch
dc	double crochet
htr	half treble
tr	treble
dtr	double treble
htr2tog	half treble 2tog
tr2tog	treble 2tog
yoh	yarn over hook
sp(s)	space(s)

Double crochet

1. Insert the hook into the work (as indicated in the pattern), wrap the yarn over the hook and draw the yarn through the work only.
2. Wrap the yarn again and draw the yarn through both loops on the hook.
3. 1 dc made

Half treble

1. Wrap the yarn over the hook & insert the hook into the work (as indicated in pattern).
2. Wrap the yarn over the hook draw through the work only and wrap the yarn again.
3. Draw through all 3 loops on the hook.
4. 1 half treble made.

Treble

1. Wrap the yarn over the hook and insert the hook into the work (as indicated on the pattern).
2. Wrap the yarn over the hook draw through the work only and wrap the yarn again.
3. Draw through the first 2 loops only and wrap the yarn again.
4. Draw through the last 2 loops on the hook.
5. 1 treble made.

ABBREVIATIONS

K	knit
P	purl
K1b	knit 1 through back loop
st(s)	stitch(es)
inc	increas(e)(ing)
dec	decreas(e)(ing)
st st	stocking stitch (1 row K, 1 row P)
garter st	garter stitch (K every row)
beg	begin(ning)
foll	following
rem	remain(ing)
rev st st	reverse stocking stitch (1 row P, 1 row K)
rep	repeat
alt	alternate
cont	continue
patt	pattern
tog	together
mm	millimetres
cm	centimetres
in(s)	inch(es)
RS	right side
WS	wrong side
sl 1	slip one stitch
psso	pass slipped stitch over
tbl	through back of loop
M1	make one stitch by picking up horizontal loop before next stitch and knitting into back of it
M1p	make one stitch by picking up horizontal loop before next stitch and purling into back of it
yfwd	yarn forward
yon	yarn over needle
yrn	yarn round needle
MP	Make picot: Cast on 1 st, by inserting the right needle between the first and second stitch on left needle, take yarn round needle, bring loop through and place on left (one stitch cast on), cast off 1 st, by knitting first the loop and then the next stitch, pass the first stitch over the second (one stitch cast off).
Cn	cable needle
C4B	Cable 4 back: Slip next 2 sts onto a cn and hold at back of work, K2, K2 from cn.
C4F	Cable 4 front: Slip next 2 sts onto a cn and hold at front of work, K2, K2 from cn.

INDEX

THANK YOU!

We would like to say a huge, enormous, whopping thank you to the following fantastic people; Graham Watts, Angela Lin, Naomi Vergette-D'Souza, Diana Fisher, Sue Whiting, Tricia McKenzie, Susan Laybourn, Ella Taylor, Sandra Richardson, Margaret Oswald, Glennis Garnet, Betty Falconer & Patricia Liddle. We are also extremely grateful to Thelma Pickford & all at the Friends Meeting House at High Flatts, Helene at Revival www.revivalvintage.co.uk, Vorriey, John & the ladies at Be Authentic, www.beauthentic. co.uk and, as always, to Kate, David, Ann & the Rowan team for their support.

We could not have done it without you.

Kim, Kathleen & Lindsay